Einkorn *Made Easy*

Einkorn
Made Easy

50 Simple Recipes for
Nature's Delicious
Low-Gluten Ancient Grain

Adrian J. S. Hale

 SASQUATCH BOOKS | SEATTLE

Contents

Recipes

53 Mains

91 Breads and Crackers

117 Sweet Treats

Introduction

In some ways, einkorn is an unlikely food to write an everyday cookbook about. It's in the category of "ancient grains," after all, which isn't exactly what comes to mind when someone says, "Come by the house Saturday for a dinner party!" or "Let's whip up something fun as an after-school snack!" or "Let's celebrate with a cake!" Einkorn, however, can be an asset in all of these situations—especially when anyone involved has a wheat sensitivity.

This ancient wheat is *the* original wheat, used by our early ancestors and found in an archaeological site that predates the development of agriculture. Unlike other ancient foods—say ferns or ptarmigan, which would be hard to incorporate into our modern diets—einkorn is timeless.

It's ancient, yes, but it's also just wheat, which we know and love. Ptarmigan-fern stew sounds like a history project or a stunt. But stuffed eggplant parm and skillet cookies? Sign me up! Today, as more and more people are finding that wheat doesn't always love us back, einkorn has found new relevance. And this is part of my own family's story.

I came to einkorn through bread baking, and I came to bread baking because when my oldest child was four, we discovered they had a sensitivity to wheat that was causing chronic stomachaches. Among the changes we made to address this was an effort to make our food healthier and less processed, and in 2010 I started baking all my family's bread. Over time, I started experimenting with different grains to get more diversity in our diet and more nutrition into each loaf.

Eventually, I landed on an everyday einkorn loaf (see page 93). Why did I turn to those loaves over and over again? Mostly it was because my family really liked them. I noticed when I made bread with regular whole wheat flour, the loaves would linger on the bread board. But when I made einkorn loaves, they got eaten right up.

My husband played a big role in einkorn's becoming such a feature of our family's table. While I nerd out on the many merits of whole foods, he could not care less about all that. For him, I'd often make white bread with just a little added whole wheat. But einkorn was different. It seemed to cast a spell on him: When I pulled the first 100 percent einkorn loaves from the oven, he dove in gleefully—that batch was gone in a flash. In fact, every member of my family gobbled these loaves up in the form of morning toast or after-school grilled cheese.

I had to admit einkorn did have a little something special. It's a sort of golden quality that tastes minerally and a little sweet all at once. When I tasted that first loaf, I thought of haystacks and fresh soil and . . . Cheez-It crackers? And there it was: einkorn's ability to marry our ancient past with today's table. I tried it as a pastry flour, and there it shone, lending cakes a soft sweetness that's hard to define. It was like it wanted to complement the ingredients it was working with rather than compete with them. It felt not like a replacement for something else but like its own fresh idea.

I've come to think of einkorn as the grandmother of wheat: She is old and wise, but she's also the grandma at the wedding who knows how to get up and dance with the teenagers. She's still fiery after all these years, and you want her around.

I can't wait to share the qualities I love about einkorn with you. It is one of the most versatile grains I use, and I'm excited to help you get some of these classics onto your table too. I hope you love cooking with einkorn as much as I do; don't hesitate to reach out to me to share your successes.

A Simple Swap for Better Gut Health

My kid struggled with chronic stomachaches as a child—which, as I mentioned, is what got me baking seriously in the first place. We ruled out celiac disease, an autoimmune disorder wherein an immune reaction is triggered when a person consumes gluten, causing damage to the small intestine. (Gluten is a protein found in wheat, and people with celiac disease can't eat it. Ever.) Our doctor also ruled out an actual

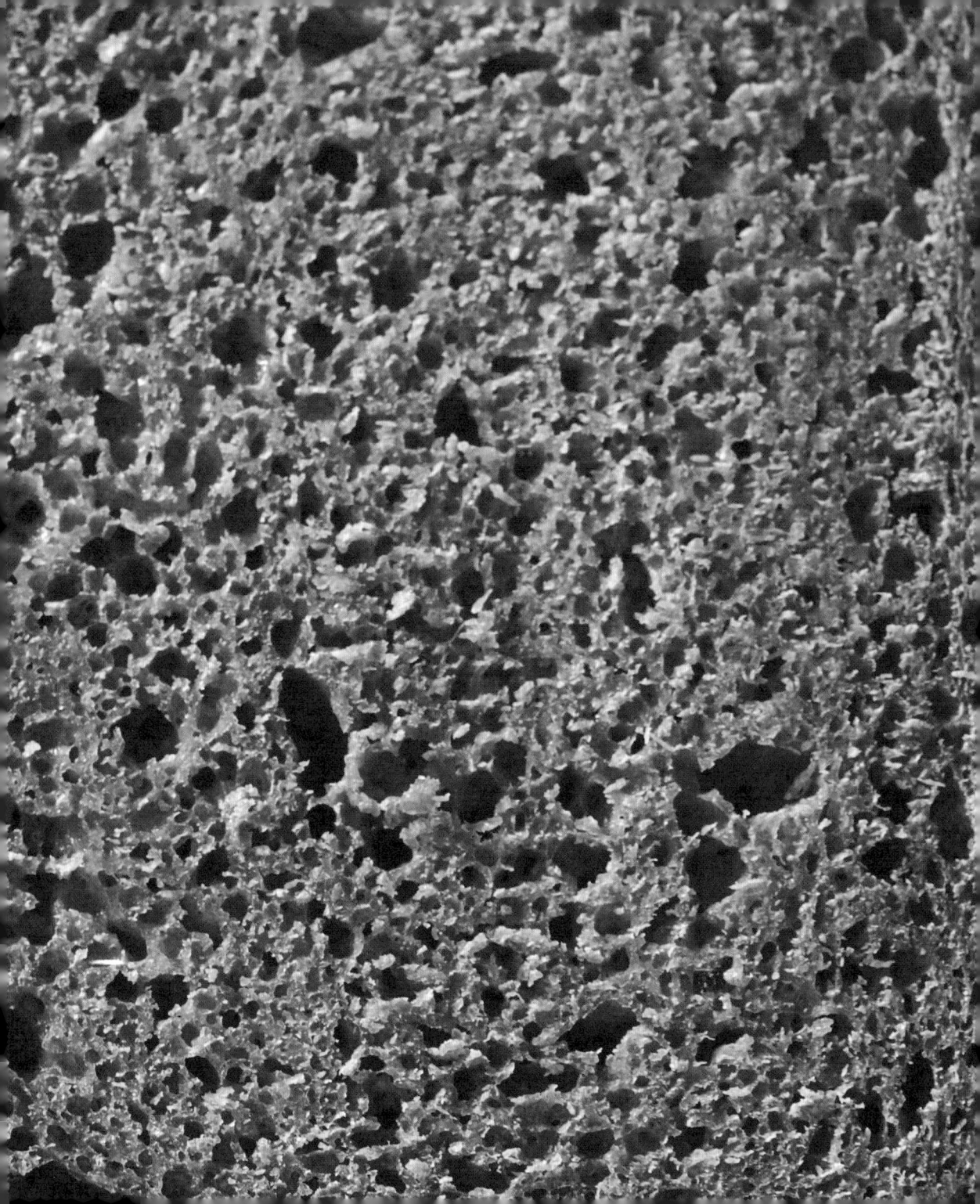

allergy but told us our kid had a "wheat sensitivity." Our first reaction was: *Huh?* My second (or maybe third) reaction was: *Hmmmm... what are the possibilities...?*

And that's how we got to know einkorn. While einkorn is a kind of wheat and does contain gluten, it tends to be a little easier on the human gut. First, einkorn has a higher proportion of bran and germ (the parts where you find the fiber) to endosperm (the part with most of the starch), giving it a better fiber profile, which in itself helps digestion. Second, it also has a different ratio of the two proteins (gliadin and glutenin) that make up gluten than modern wheat does.

The mechanisms that cause wheat intolerance (celiac disease), wheat allergy, and wheat sensitivity are not yet fully understood by scientists (and since they are different syndromes, they likely have different causes). If you have celiac disease, you shouldn't eat einkorn—it's still wheat, even though it's genetically different from modern wheats and has a healthier nutritional profile. The same is true if you have a wheat allergy: Einkorn might not be quite as harsh on your system as more modern wheats, but the research is not yet conclusive. If what you have is a nonceliac gluten sensitivity—like my kid does—einkorn may well be much easier on your digestion.

Here are some very cool things I've come to know about einkorn's nutritional profile:

- **PROTEIN PRO** It's up to 40 percent higher in protein than modern wheat. Not only that, but as I mentioned, the endosperm (the sugar-bomb part of the wheat berry) is naturally a little smaller (since einkorn hasn't been so intensively bred for yield).
- **IRON PUMPER** It's significantly higher in iron than modern and industrialized wheats, and higher in zinc and manganese as well.
- **MINERAL MARVEL** It has half the phytic acid of modern and industrialized wheats. Found in many seeds (including legumes), phytic acid is responsible for storing phosphorus in a plant. In our guts, though, phytic acid binds with minerals we need, making them unavailable for our bodies to use. For that reason, phytic acid is sometimes called an "antinutrient." (That's too simplistic, though: A little phytic acid can be a good thing, helping lower blood sugar and cholesterol.)

Two ways to lower the phytic acid levels in foods (like wheat) are fermentation and germination (sprouting). But if we want to make quick breads and cookies, those processes aren't easy to incorporate. Einkorn is a great swap-in for wheat in these kinds of recipes, reducing nutrient-stealing phytic acid without sacrificing ease or deliciousness.

- **ANTIOXIDANT CHAMPION** It has more beta-carotenes and carotenoids than other wheats (its significantly higher levels of beta-carotenes give it a yellowish hue). Beta-carotenes are a precursor to vitamin A, and they promote skin health, boost our immune systems, and help our bodies combat oxidative stress. Einkorn is especially high in the carotenoids lutein and zeaxanthin, which are both strong antioxidants and especially good for eye health.

In a world full of nutritionally empty white flour, I love being able to swap some of this ancient-grain nutrition back in by using einkorn in my cooking and baking (and it doesn't hurt that this grain tastes so good).

All About Einkorn

Of all the questions I get about einkorn, the first is (always, inevitably) some version of "What the heck is einkorn?" Many people think I'm talking about a type of corn. Understandable. When I explain that it's actually a type of wheat, and really *the* original type of wheat, they tend to look, well, even more confused.

Einkorn's history is so lengthy that even its name has ancient roots. Our word for corn (a.k.a. maize; botanical name *Zea mays*) comes from *korn*, an old German word for grain. Ein means "one" in German, so *einkorn* translates to "one grain," which probably refers to the one seed within each husk on the heads of einkorn stalks. Einkorn's botanical name is *Triticum monococcum—Triticum* being the genus name for wheat. Thus, einkorn is a type of wheat, one with a simpler genetic makeup than modern wheat types.

Don't get me wrong, I'm a fan of modern wheat. But I have fallen head over heels for einkorn. It's very ancient and—because of its nutritional profile—very modern at the same time, which is fascinating. And it gives me an easy way to pack more nutritional punch into many beloved everyday dishes—making familiar foods like the ones featured in this cookbook part of a more diversified diet.

A Little History

Einkorn is called *farro piccolo* in Italian and *petit épeautre* in French: Both mean "little spelt." My favorite translation is the Greek *tiphe*, which might be a mistranslation of the word for *tithe* (a tax or levy). Turkey might have the longest history of eating einkorn (*siyez*, in Turkish); it's cultivated in the forested areas of northern Turkey near the Black Sea.

People may like to bandy about the term "ancient grain," but einkorn is the grandmother to other wheats we call "ancient." Archaeologists discovered it in fossilized pieces of bread that were dated to about four thousand years before humans began farming. These fossils show that our hunter-gatherer ancestors were eating einkorn bread and maybe even throwing big feasts where einkorn bread was a mainstay. We also know that Ötzi, the Bronze-Age man found mummified under a glacier on the border of Italy and Austria, ate einkorn right before he died.

The wheat we eat today is very different. About eight thousand years ago, a "polyploidization event" occurred with wheat. That sounds like another name for a rave, if you ask me. And in a way, it was a kind of love-in, during which ancient wheats came together with goat grasses, merging genomes and creating new, more genetically complex species. So while einkorn has fourteen chromosomes, emmer and durum each have twenty-eight, and modern wheats have forty-two. In and of itself, these changes are not a bad thing, but the more modern wheats seem to trigger immune responses in some people.

Using the Recipes in This Book

The chapters that follow are organized by type of dish or meal (morning foods, lighter soup-and-salad meals, main dishes, breads and crackers, and sweets). I tested all the recipes in this book with whole grain einkorn flour as it's the easiest kind to get. There are many high-quality einkorn flours on the market, but only one reliable source of white einkorn flour (a flour from which the grain's bran and germ are removed). I have also found that I prefer the taste of whole grain cookies, brownies, and cakes.

I tested several recipes with both white and whole grain einkorn flours, but there are only a few instances where I would maybe consider (and I really mean *maybe*) trading the amazing health benefits of whole grain for the texture of white flour. The pasta on page 79 and the biscuits on page 99 are the two recipes in this book that incorporate the flour in a way that allows you to adjust as you go to ensure you're achieving the right texture—so start there if you want to experiment.

Measuring Flour and Other Dry Ingredients for Baked Goods

When I bake, I weigh the main dry and liquid ingredients in my batters and doughs to get the most precise results. I am also aware that many home bakers are more comfortable using volume measurements and may not have or use a kitchen scale. So while using weight measures is my preference, I tested these recipes using volume measures as well and have provided weight equivalents only for dry ingredients that make up a dough or batter. I measure volume by scooping the ingredient (such as flour or sugar) into a measuring spoon or cup without packing it down and then level the top with the straight edge of a butter knife. For brown sugar, I indicate in the recipes whether to pack it or not.

Swapping In White Einkorn Flour for Whole Grain: The Math

White flour absorbs less liquid than whole wheat flour does. So, as a rule, if you want to use white flour rather than the whole grain flour called for in a recipe, adjust the liquid in the recipe to use from 75 percent to 88 percent of the water called for. Start with 75 percent: For example, if I call for 2 cups of liquid in a whole wheat flour recipe, incorporate 1½ cups of liquid in the white-flour version, then add more if needed to bring the batter or dough to the consistency specified in the recipe.

Tips on Working with Einkorn

Working with einkorn is different in some ways than working with other flours or whole grains. Some differences are simpler to adjust for, and some are trickier (most of these have to do with yeasted baked goods).

When cooking whole berries, you'll find they cook up quickly compared to many other grains. If you substitute einkorn berries for other grains in casseroles and soups, you'll want to take that into account.

Substituting einkorn for standard wheat flours in quick breads and cookies is pretty straightforward and doesn't require much adjustment in technique. Once you make some of the recipes in this book, you'll get a sense of how einkorn behaves in these more forgiving types of recipe.

Yeasted bread recipes are where it gets a bit more complicated. When making einkorn breads that require any kind of fermentation, it's necessary to pay close attention. Fermentation times can vary because although whole grains absorb water more slowly, ancient grains tend to have more enzymatic activity which speeds up some of the fermentation processes. This can lead to a faster degradation of gluten and starch development if you let them go too long at room temperature. This means the dough might become stickier, which is especially true of einkorn. It's a balance of getting the right amount of water, but making sure you don't overhydrate the dough or it will become a mess to work with. I have tackled this issue by giving the fermented breads long proofs in the refrigerator, which helps ease this tricky phenomenon.

Notes on Ingredients

These ingredients and staples are nice to have on hand as you make the recipes in this book.

BROTH: I often make broth from scratch at home, and if you do too, feel free to use it in recipes where it's called for. For store-bought, I recommend Better than Bouillon bases, including their vegetable-based No Chicken flavor, which you can use to make a quick vegetarian broth.

DAIRY: Unless otherwise specified, these recipes use full-fat dairy. I tested many of them (such as the cheater bagels on page 109) with lower-fat versions, and if I did, I mention that in the headnote. I also give vegan alternatives where I can.

EGGS: All recipes that call for eggs use large eggs.

EINKORN BERRIES AND WHOLE GRAIN FLOUR: Bluebird Grain Farms, Camas Country Mill, Carolina Ground, Janie's Mill, and Maine Grains are all good sources for einkorn berries and flour. Einkorn flour is becoming more common at standard grocers, but you can generally find these brands at your local natural food store or online.

EINKORN FLOUR (WHITE): Jovial Foods' white (all-purpose) einkorn flour is readily available at most natural food stores or online. If you're switching out white flour for whole wheat flour, or vice versa, see page 10 for advice about adjustments to liquid measures.

OILS: Olive oil is always extra-virgin, and sunflower oil is my favorite neutral tasting oil (though whatever neutral oil you have in your pantry will work just fine).

PASTA: Jovial makes einkorn pasta that is great for a ready-made pasta. My favorite off-the-shelf einkorn pasta is made by Sfoglini, although it's not 100 percent einkorn flour. Both can be purchased online and in many supermarkets.

SALT: Unless otherwise specified, all these recipes are made with kosher salt.

Milling Grain at Home

You don't need to mill your own grain at home to use this book. But if you're up for it, milling your own wheat gives you control over the fineness of the grind and the freshness of the flavor. Though I often buy flour already ground, I usually keep a 25-pound bag of Bluebird whole einkorn in my pantry and grind it myself. My mill is the KoMo Classic, and I've had it for years.

Equipment

For the recipes in this book, you'll need just a few standard kitchen tools.

- A food processor or blender and a stand mixer or a good old-fashioned electric hand mixer
- A Dutch oven or an oven-safe equivalent
- An 8-by-8-inch brownie pan, an 8-by-4-inch loaf pan, a 9-by-13-inch casserole pan, 9-inch cake pan, baking sheets, and half sheet pans
- A pullman pan, if you have one, is handy for making the sandwich bread on page 93; alternatively, an 8½-by-4½-inch loaf pan will do.

Storage

To store einkorn, I get big Cambro storage containers from the restaurant supply store and wash them between uses. A Cambro is basically a durable restaurant-grade storage container. Each time I finish a batch, I wash the Cambro well with hot soapy water and let it dry fully before filling it back up. I also keep a little bay leaves nearby because I've heard that it will somewhat repel pantry moths and such. So far so good, but I'm definitely knocking on wood. I keep the area around my grain containers very clean and dry at all times.

Keeping Flour Fresh

Use already-ground whole grain flour within a month. Ideally, store it in the freezer to keep the oils from the germ fresh for longer.

Morning Meals

Dutch Baby Pancake
with Orange-Almond Sugar

A 10-inch cast-iron pan is ideal for this recipe, but if you don't have one, a stainless-steel pan will do just fine as long as it's oven-safe. Bring the eggs to room temperature before using.

MAKES 2 TO 4 SERVINGS

For the topping
½ cup sugar
Zest of 1 medium orange, chopped
  (about 1 tablespoon)
Pinch of kosher salt
2 tablespoons whole almonds, toasted

For the pancake
¾ cup (90 grams) whole grain
  einkorn flour
¼ teaspoon ground cinnamon
¼ teaspoon ground nutmeg
¼ teaspoon kosher salt
3 eggs, at room temperature
¾ cup whole milk
½ teaspoon vanilla extract
3 tablespoons unsalted butter

1   Put a 10-inch cast-iron pan on the middle rack of the oven and preheat to 450 degrees F.

2   To make the topping, mix the sugar, orange zest, and salt in a small bowl. Finely chop the toasted almonds and mix them into the sugar mixture. Cover the bowl and set it on the table; the flavors will develop while you prepare the pancake.

3   To make the pancake, sift the flour, cinnamon, nutmeg, and salt into a small bowl. In a separate, large bowl, beat the eggs with a whisk or electric beater until they're pale and airy. Add the milk and vanilla and beat until you see frothy bubbles. Stir the flour mixture into the liquid ingredients just until combined.

4   Acting quickly, pull the hot cast-iron pan out of the oven and put the butter into the pan. As soon as the butter has melted and starts to brown, pour the pancake batter into the pan and return it to the oven. Bake for about 15 minutes, until the dough puffs up in rumpled, irregular waves. There should be little streams of butter running through the peaks and valleys of the pancake.

5   Get the baby to the table right away. Cut it into wedges and serve it right out of the pan. Pass around the orange-almond sugar so people can help themselves.

Whole Grain Waffles

I created these waffles with a vegan friend in mind. Feel free to use whatever milk you have on hand—plant-based or otherwise. Any will work to make this tasty and hearty breakfast treat. My waffle iron makes 6-inch waffles and uses about 1/3 cup batter per waffle. You might have to sacrifice your first waffle to figure out how much batter and how many minutes your waffle iron needs to produce perfect golden-brown goodness.

MAKES TEN TO TWELVE 6-INCH WAFFLES

3 cups (360 grams) whole grain einkorn flour
¼ cup (45 grams) granulated sugar
1 tablespoon baking powder
1 tablespoon flax meal
½ teaspoon kosher salt
3 cups whole dairy milk or plant-based milk

½ cup sunflower oil or other neutral oil
¼ cup applesauce
1 tablespoon freshly squeezed lemon juice
Nonstick cooking spray
Butter (or vegan butter), maple syrup, jam, and/or confectioners' sugar, for serving

1   Preheat the waffle iron while you make the batter.

2   In a medium bowl, stir the flour, sugar, baking powder, flax meal, and salt together. In a large jug or bowl (ideally one with a spout for easy pouring), whisk the milk, oil, applesauce, and lemon juice together. When the mixture is well combined and a little foam forms around the edges from whisking the eggs, add the dry ingredients to the jug and mix until just combined (it's okay if the batter is a little lumpy).

3   Spray the hot waffle iron with cooking spray, pour enough batter into the iron to just fill the bottom plate (don't overfill or batter will squeeze out the sides), and close the lid. After about 4 minutes, check the edges of the waffle peeking out between the plates; if they're nicely browned and a little crispy, the waffle is ready.

4   It's best to eat these straight from the iron, but if you need to hold them for a bit, put them in the oven on low (200 degrees F) to keep them warm. Serve with your choice of butter (or a plant-based buttery spread), maple syrup, jam, and/or sugar.

Cherry Buttermilk Breakfast Loaf

This loaf makes a good breakfast for busy families, but it's equally delightful as an afternoon snack. Feel free to switch out the cherries for another seasonal fruit like peaches or plums; you can even use fruit straight from the freezer.

MAKES ONE 8-INCH LOAF

¼ cup (½ stick) unsalted butter, cubed, plus softened butter to grease the pan (and, optionally, more for serving)
2 cups (240 g) plus 1 tablespoon whole grain einkorn flour
½ cup (90 g) sugar
2 teaspoons baking powder

½ teaspoon baking soda
1 teaspoon kosher salt
1 egg
1 cup buttermilk
½ cup halved pitted fresh or frozen cherries
Cream cheese, for serving (optional)

1   Preheat the oven to 350 degrees F.

2   In a small pan over low heat, melt the cubed butter, then set aside to cool. Grease the bottom and sides of an 8-by-4-inch loaf pan with softened butter and set aside.

3   In a large mixing bowl, stir together the 2 cups of einkorn flour, sugar, baking powder, and baking soda. In a separate, medium bowl, beat the egg and mix in the buttermilk. Stir the wet ingredients into the dry ingredients, then stir in the melted butter until it's incorporated and no longer streaky. In a small bowl, toss the cherries in the remaining 1 tablespoon flour until they're coated and stir them into the batter just until they're dispersed in the batter (don't overmix).

4   Scrape the batter into the prepared loaf pan and set the pan in the middle of the oven. Bake for 50 minutes, turning the pan halfway through the cooking time. Remove when a toothpick inserted into the center comes out clean. Let the loaf cool in the pan for about 10 minutes, then turn it out onto a board and slice thickly. To serve, spread the warm slices with butter or cream cheese as you like. The loaf will keep tightly wrapped at room temperature for about a week.

Maple-Pecan Porridge

I love a simple porridge, but einkorn flakes are hard to come by. Luckily, you can make this porridge with whole einkorn berries by cracking the grain in a blender for a flavor and texture that would tempt Goldilocks.

MAKES 2 SERVINGS

½ cup einkorn berries
1 cup water
¼ cup maple syrup, plus more
 for drizzling

1 tablespoon unsalted butter
¼ teaspoon ground cinnamon
¼ cup pecan halves, toasted

1   In a blender or food processor, pulse the einkorn berries for about 30 seconds to crack the grain. In a small saucepan, combine the water and maple syrup. Over medium-high heat, bring to a boil, stirring a few times to keep the grain from sticking to the bottom. Turn the heat to the lowest level, cover the pan, and simmer for 25 minutes, until the grain is thick and porridge-like. Remove from the heat and stir in the butter and cinnamon.

2   Transfer to two bowls and top with toasted pecans. Drizzle with more maple syrup to taste.

Peanut Butter–Filled Chocolate Morning Muffins

I owe this recipe to my son, who thought these muffins up when he was in kindergarten. I still make them, but now they greet him on his return from varsity football practice instead of on his way to learn his ABCs. Cradle one of these warm muffins in your hands on a cold morning or dunk one in coffee or a glass of cold milk. Use whatever peanut butter you have on hand. I butter the cups of my muffin tin for this one instead of using liners—I love the little bits of peanut butter peeking out the sides of the muffins.

MAKES 1 DOZEN MUFFINS

¾ cup peanut butter

2 cups (240 grams) whole grain einkorn flour

1¼ cups (250 grams) packed brown sugar

½ cup (45 grams) cocoa powder

1 teaspoon baking soda

½ teaspoon kosher salt

2 eggs

½ cup sunflower oil or other neutral oil

¾ cup whole milk

¾ cup sour cream

2 teaspoons vanilla extract

½ cup bittersweet chocolate chips (optional)

1 tablespoon confectioners' sugar

1. Preheat the oven to 350 degrees F. Butter the cups of a standard muffin pan or line them with paper liners.

2. Line a small plate or quarter sheet pan with parchment paper and divide the peanut butter into twelve tablespoon-size dollops. Put the plate in the freezer to chill.

3. In a medium bowl, whisk together the einkorn flour, brown sugar, cocoa powder, baking soda, and salt.

4. In a large bowl, beat the eggs with a whisk until they're a bit frothy. Drizzle in the oil, continuing to beat until emulsified, then add the milk, sour cream, and vanilla, beating to combine after each addition.

$\longrightarrow$

5   With a spatula, fold the dry ingredients into the wet ingredients just until there are no visible streaks of flour. Finally, stir in the chocolate chips. Let the batter rest for 10 minutes or so.

6   Put the confectioners' sugar on a small plate. Take the peanut butter dollops out of the freezer and roll them in the sugar.

7   Scoop about 3 tablespoons of batter into each muffin cup to fill halfway. Place one of the frozen peanut butter balls into each muffin cup and cover with more batter, until about three-quarters filled (the muffins will rise as they bake).

8   Bake for 25 minutes, rotating the pan halfway through the cooking time. Remove from the oven when a toothpick inserted into the center comes out clean or with only a few crumbs. Set the pan on a wire rack to cool for about 10 minutes, then invert the muffins onto the rack to cool until warm but not too hot to eat (they're outstanding served warm).

9   Store the muffins in an airtight container at room temperature for about 3 days, or freeze, tightly wrapped, for up to a month. If you freeze them, warm them by popping them in the oven for 5 to 10 minutes at 350 degrees F.

Cinnamon Coffee Cake
with Streusel Topping

This is the coffee cake recipe to have on hand for brunches and afternoon tea alike; it's also lovely for a simple breakfast, served warm with coffee. You can whip it up in no time, and it uses simple pantry ingredients you probably have on hand.

MAKES 4 TO 6 SERVINGS

For the streusel topping
¾ cup brown sugar
¾ cup whole grain einkorn flour
1 tablespoon ground cinnamon
½ cup (1 stick) cold unsalted butter

For the cake
1½ cups (180 grams) whole grain
  einkorn flour
1½ teaspoons baking powder

¾ teaspoon kosher salt
¼ teaspoon baking soda
¾ cup (135 grams) sugar
½ cup (1 stick) unsalted butter,
  softened, plus more for the pan
2 eggs
1 cup sour cream
2 tablespoons whole milk
1 teaspoon vanilla extract

1   Preheat the oven to 350 degrees F.

2   To make the streusel topping, in a medium bowl, combine the brown sugar, einkorn flour, and cinnamon. Stir to mix well. Using a pastry cutter or food processor, cut the cold butter into the sugar and flour until the mixture looks like wet sand. Store the bowl in the refrigerator until ready to use.

3   To make the cake, in a medium bowl, combine the flour, baking powder, salt, and baking soda. Stir to mix well.

4   In a large bowl with a hand mixer or in the bowl of a stand mixer fitted with the paddle attachment, beat the sugar and softened butter together on medium-high speed until it starts to look fluffy, 2 to 3 minutes. Beat in the eggs one by one, then the sour cream, milk, and vanilla. Mix well to incorporate everything. Add the flour mixture about a third at a time, mixing just until there's no dry flour.

$\longrightarrow$

5 Lightly grease an 8-inch round baking pan. Spread half the batter in the pan. Retrieve the streusel topping from the fridge and sprinkle two-thirds of it over the batter. Dollop spoonfuls of the remaining batter on top of the streusel, trying to cover most of the surface. Don't try to spread the batter around (the topping will keep it from spreading) and don't worry if you miss a spot or two. Sprinkle the remaining third of the streusel on top.

6 Bake for 30 to 40 minutes, until a toothpick inserted into the center comes out clean. Let cool for at least 10 minutes before slicing. Keeps tightly wrapped at room temperature for up to a week.

Candied-Ginger Einkorn Scones

I have a friend who hosts a yearly holiday brunch at Easter, and candied ginger scones are always on the menu. I look forward to them every year, and I was delighted to discover they're even better with einkorn flour. The key to making a good scone is to keepthe dough as cold as possible and to use a light hand while you're working the dough (overworking it can lead to tough scones).

MAKES 8 SCONES

2 cups (240 grams) whole grain einkorn flour

½ cup (100 grams) packed brown sugar

1 tablespoon baking powder

½ teaspoon ground ginger

½ teaspoon kosher salt

1 egg

½ cup heavy cream, plus more for brushing the tops

2 teaspoons vanilla extract

½ cup (1 stick) unsalted butter, frozen

1 cup diced candied ginger

Sanding sugar or granulated sugar, for topping

1   Line a baking sheet with a silicone baking mat or parchment paper.

2   In a large bowl, whisk together the einkorn flour, brown sugar, baking powder, ginger, and salt. Put these dry ingredients in the fridge or freezer to chill.

3   In a medium bowl, beat the egg, then mix in the heavy cream and vanilla. Put the bowl in the fridge to chill.

4   Using the largest holes on a box grater, grate the stick of frozen butter into a shallow bowl. Retrieve the bowl of dry ingredients from the fridge or freezer and add the butter. In a food processor or using a pastry cutter, cut the butter into the dry ingredients until everything looks like wet sand with a few pea-size pieces. If using a food processor, pulse just enough to get the right consistency—don't overwork it!

$\longrightarrow$

5   Add the candied ginger and cut in or pulse just until it's diffused throughout the dough mixture. Take the wet ingredients from the fridge and pour slowly into the dry ingredients, pulsing or mixing with a spatula until the dough just comes together.

6   Turn the dough out onto a clean work surface and bring it together into a rough ball, turning once or twice so everything holds together. Pat it into a disk about 5 inches across and ¾- to 1-inch thick and cut into eight wedges. Arrange the wedges on the lined baking sheet and put in the refrigerator for at least 10 minutes and up to overnight.

7   Move a rack to the middle of the oven and preheat to 400 degrees F. Remove the scones from the fridge and brush their tops with a bit of heavy cream; sprinkle with sanding sugar. Bake for 15 to 18 minutes, until the tops of the scones are browned and they spring back when you press on them. Serve scones the same day.

Scrambled Eggs and Gravy-Smothered Biscuits

This recipe is a mash-up of breakfast classics (scrambled eggs, biscuits, and sausage gravy) that turns the dial up to eleven. It's a go-hard gut-buster of a way to start your day. I call for chicken sausage here, but you can substitute sautéed sliced mushrooms for all or part of the sausage—in fact, I recommend you try it that way at least once. You'll want to pop the freezer biscuits (see page 99) into the oven about twenty minutes before you plan to eat so they're warm and ready at the same time as the gravy and eggs.

MAKES 4 SERVINGS

3 tablespoons unsalted butter, divided
1 pound bulk chicken sausage
¼ cup whole grain einkorn flour
2½ cups whole milk
Kosher salt and freshly ground black pepper
4 eggs
4 Make-Ahead Einkorn Freezer Biscuits (page 99) or store-bought freezer biscuits, freshly baked

8 slices (8 to 12 ounces, depending on thickness) smoked turkey breast (optional)
4 to 5 cups (4 ounces) loosely packed spinach or arugula
3 green onions, green parts only, thinly sliced

$\longrightarrow$

1   In a large skillet over medium-high heat, melt 2 tablespoons of the butter. Add the sausage in chunks and stir to keep breaking it up into small pieces as it cooks. Cook until it's nice and browned, 3 to 5 minutes, then sprinkle over the flour and stir to coat everything. Continue cooking and stirring for about 5 minutes, then slowly pour in the milk, whisking to eliminate any lumps. Keep whisking while the mixture comes to a simmer. Lower the heat and continue to simmer, uncovered, until the gravy thickens up, about 10 minutes. Add salt and pepper to taste. Remove from the heat and cover while you prepare the eggs.

2   Crack the eggs into a medium bowl and whisk them with a fork. In a medium saucepan over medium-high heat, melt the remaining tablespoon of butter. Pour in the eggs and cook, stirring, until they're softly scrambled, about 4 minutes.

3   To serve, open the biscuits and lay two halves on each of four plates. Place a slice of smoked turkey on each biscuit half, top with a bit of fresh spinach or arugula, then spoon over some of the softly scrambled eggs. Smother the whole thing with sausage gravy and sprinkle with sliced green onions.

Soups
AND
Salads

Einkorn and Kale Salad

with Harissa Dressing

This is probably my favorite salad recipe of all time. If you make it, I think you'll understand why. Harissa, a North African chili paste, makes up the base of this dressing; the paste is easy to make from scratch, but there are many good store-bought ones. If you substitute ready-made harissa, you'll need about 2 tablespoons. This salad tastes great the day you make it, but it lasts so well in the fridge that you can eat it for the whole week.

MAKES 6 TO 8 SERVINGS

½ cup einkorn berries

For the harissa
2 teaspoons ground cumin
1½ teaspoons kosher salt, plus more
    as needed
1 teaspoon sweet paprika
¼ teaspoon ground coriander
¼ teaspoon ground Aleppo pepper or
    chili powder
3 cloves garlic, minced
2 teaspoons freshly squeezed lemon
    juice, plus more as needed
1 teaspoon tomato paste
Pinch of sugar, plus more as needed

For the salad
1 bunch lacinato (Tuscan) kale
1½ tablespoons sherry vinegar
¾ cup extra-virgin olive oil
1½ cups slivered almonds, toasted
¾ cup chopped dried apricots
4 ounces feta, crumbled

1   In a medium saucepan, combine the einkorn berries with water to cover by 2 inches. Bring to a rolling boil, lower the heat to medium-high, and cook for 20 to 25 minutes, skimming the foam from time to time, until the einkorn grains are softened and have started to split open. Drain in a sieve and rinse with cold water. Set aside to cool completely.

2   To make the harissa paste, in a medium bowl, combine the cumin, salt, paprika, coriander, Aleppo pepper, garlic, lemon juice, tomato paste, and sugar. Stir together, then let sit for about 20 minutes for the flavors to combine.

3 To prepare the salad, wash the kale and cut the tough stems and center ribs from each leaf. Cut the leaves into thin ribbons, adding them to a salad bowl as you work. Add the cooled einkorn and toss to combine.

4 Stir the vinegar into the harissa. Drizzle the olive oil into the harissa–vinegar mixture in a slow, steady stream, whisking continuously to emulsify the dressing. Pour it over the kale and einkorn and toss well. Add the almonds, dried apricots, and feta and mix until every bite gets a bit of everything. Taste and adjust seasonings, adding a bit more salt, sugar, or lemon as needed, and serve (or refrigerate until ready to serve, up to a week).

Waldorf Salad

This salad is refreshing any time of year, but I especially turn to it in the colder months, when I'm missing the bounty of a summertime farmer's market. It features a few simple ingredients that are available all year and has even made it onto our Thanksgiving menu, where it brings a welcome freshness to the table.

MAKES 4 TO 6 SERVINGS

¼ cup einkorn berries

For the dressing
2 tablespoons sour cream
1 tablespoon freshly squeezed
   lemon juice
1 tablespoon mayonnaise
2 teaspoons honey
¼ teaspoon kosher salt
Freshly ground black pepper

For the salad
1 medium Granny Smith apple
1 medium stalk celery, diced
½ cup (about 10) red grapes, halved
1 tablespoon chopped parsley leaves
1 tablespoon chopped fresh dill
½ cup walnut pieces, toasted

1   In a small pot over high heat, bring 2 inches of water to a boil and add the einkorn berries (the water should cover the einkorn by at least an inch). When the water has returned to a rolling boil, lower the heat to medium-high and cook for 20 to 25 minutes, skimming the foam from time to time, until the einkorn grains are softened and have started to split open. Drain in a sieve and rinse with cold water Set aside to cool.

2   To prepare the dressing, in a small bowl, whisk together the sour cream, lemon juice, mayonnaise, honey, salt, and several grinds of pepper. Taste and adjust the seasonings and set aside.

3   To make the salad, dice the apple and add it to a serving bowl along with the cooled einkorn, celery, grapes, parsley, and dill. Pour over the dressing and toss to coat everything well.

4   Add the walnuts just before serving. If you don't finish it all in one sitting, the salad will last for a few days in the fridge.

Greek Crunch Salad

This satisfying salad is a complete meal—packed with protein and united by a tangy, herby dressing. Put any leftovers in a mason jar to take to work; the salad will keep in the fridge for a day or two (it just won't be as crunchy).

MAKES 4 TO 6 SERVINGS

For the crunch topping
1 cup cooked einkorn berries,
    drained well and cooled
1 (15-ounce) can chickpeas,
    drained well
2 tablespoons extra-virgin olive oil
½ teaspoon kosher salt

For the dressing
¼ cup extra-virgin olive oil
2 tablespoons red wine vinegar
1 tablespoon freshly squeezed
    lemon juice
½ teaspoon Dijon mustard

1 clove garlic, minced
½ teaspoon dried oregano
½ teaspoon kosher salt
Freshly ground black pepper

For the salad
1 pint cherry tomatoes, halved
3 Persian cucumbers, diced
½ small red onion, diced
1 small red pepper, diced
1 (2-ounce) can sliced black or
    kalamata olives
½ cup (2 ounces) feta, crumbled
3 or 4 fresh mint leaves, slivered

1 To prepare the crunchy topping, preheat the oven to 425 degrees F. In a medium bowl, combine the einkorn, chickpeas, olive oil, and salt and mix well so that the einkorn and chickpeas are coated. Spread the mixture on a baking sheet in a single layer and roast for 30 minutes, stirring every 10 minutes to prevent burning. Set aside to cool for a few minutes.

2 While the topping cooks, make the dressing: In a small bowl, whisk the olive oil, vinegar, lemon juice, and mustard together until well combined. Add the garlic, oregano, and salt and whisk to combine. Add a grind or two of pepper, adjust the seasonings to taste, and put aside.

3 To make the salad, in a large serving bowl, combine the tomatoes, cucumbers, onion, red pepper, sliced olives, and feta and toss together. Scatter the crunchy topping and fresh mint over the salad and serve.

Tomato Bread Soup

I'd been looking for a tomato soup for a long time, trying every one I came across in search of the perfect balance of flavors and textures. One day, before cookbook club, I pulled out a treasured book that's been on my shelf for over a decade. It contained, of course, the creamy tomato soup I'd been looking for the whole time. The secret isn't cream or coconut milk—it's bread! This tomato soup is inspired by that recipe but uses einkorn bread as a thickener. It beats all others, plus I can serve it to my vegan friends.

MAKES 4 TO 6 SERVINGS

1 (28-ounce) can peeled whole tomatoes (with or without basil)

2 tablespoons extra-virgin olive oil

1 medium yellow onion, diced

3 cloves garlic, minced

1 teaspoon ground cumin

1 (14.5-ounce) can diced tomatoes with green chilies

3 cups vegetable broth or chicken broth

1 slice Einkorn Bread (page 93) or Versatile Pita Bread (page 103) or store-bought

1 tablespoon honey

Fresh herbs (such as cilantro, basil, or mint), for garnish

1   Empty the can of whole tomatoes into a medium bowl and crush them with your hands until they start to break down. Set aside.

2   In a large pot over medium heat, heat the olive oil until shimmering. Add the onion and cook for 5 minutes, until it's just starting to get some color. Add the garlic and cumin and cook for 30 seconds more, stirring. Add both types of tomatoes to the pot. Scrape the bottom of the pot to dislodge anything that may be sticking, add the broth, and bring to a simmer. Cover the pot, turn the heat to medium-low, and simmer for 20 minutes.

3   Tear the bread into three or four pieces and add these to the pot along with the honey. Stir and cook uncovered for 10 more minutes.

4   Cool slightly, then carefully transfer about three-quarters of the soup—including all the pieces of bread—to a blender and blend until smooth. Return the blended soup to the pot, stir to combine with the chunky portion of the soup, and taste to adjust the seasonings. Bring back to a simmer and serve hot, scattering each serving with fresh herbs.

Weeknight Sausage and Savoy Cabbage Soup

This soup captures the flavors of my childhood: Both the Italian and the Jewish parts of my family ate cabbage in different ways. This soup marries both together—and it's simple to put together on a weeknight. For me, it's comfort in a bowl.

MAKES 4 MAIN-COURSE SERVINGS OR 8 APPETIZER SERVINGS

2 teaspoons extra-virgin olive oil
1½ pounds sweet Italian sausage, either chicken or pork
3 medium celery stalks, diced
2 medium carrots, diced
1 small yellow onion, diced
¾ cup einkorn berries
4 cups high-quality chicken broth

4 cups water
1 small head of savoy cabbage (1 to 1½ pounds), shredded
1 teaspoon white wine vinegar
Kosher salt and freshly ground black pepper
Parmesan cheese, for serving (optional)

1   In a large Dutch oven or heavy pot over medium heat, heat the olive oil until shimmering. Add the sausage in chunks and stir, breaking it up into small pieces as it cooks. Cook for about 5 minutes, until it's mostly cooked through and starting to brown on the edges. Add the celery, carrots, and onion and cook until they start to soften and the onion begins to look translucent, 5 to 8 minutes. Add the einkorn berries and stir until they are completely incorporated into the mixture and coated with oil.

2   Add the chicken broth and water and scrape all the bits off the bottom of the pot as the liquid heats to a boil. Cover and lower the heat to keep the soup at a simmer. Cook for 30 minutes, until the einkorn is barely tender. Add the cabbage, cover, and cook for 20 minutes more, until the cabbage has softened.

3   Stir in the vinegar and add salt and pepper as needed to taste. Serve hot, grating over as much Parmesan cheese as you like.

Minestrone

with a Shower of Parmesan

This soup is perfect for summer—especially when the garden is overflowing with zucchini. It's simple and light but nutritionally rich. Use vegetable broth and skip the Parmesan garnish to make it vegan.

MAKES 4 TO 6 SERVINGS

2 tablespoons extra-virgin olive oil
1 large yellow onion, diced
Kosher salt
2 medium carrots, diced
2 medium stalks celery, diced
1 large zucchini, diced
8 cloves garlic, sliced
1 cup einkorn berries

1 (10-ounce) can diced tomatoes
6 cups chicken broth or
    vegetable broth
Freshly ground black pepper
Chopped fresh basil leaves or pesto,
    for serving
½ cup shredded Parmesan cheese,
    divided (optional)

1   In a large pot or Dutch oven over medium heat, warm the olive oil. Add the onion and cook for 3 to 5 minutes, stirring once or twice. Add about ½ teaspoon of salt to help pull liquid out of the vegetables. When the onion starts to become translucent and smell sweet, add the carrots, celery, and zucchini. Cook until these are just starting to soften, stirring occasionally so the mixture doesn't brown. (You don't want any of the vegetables to get color; you're just sweating them a bit to concentrate the flavors.) Add the garlic and cook, stirring, for about 1 minute, until fragrant. Add the einkorn berries and stir to coat with the oil, then add the diced tomatoes and, as the liquid heats, scrape and stir to loosen any bits at the bottom of the pot. Add the broth, turn the heat to high, and bring to a quick boil. Decrease the heat to medium-low, cover, and simmer for 35 minutes.

2   When the einkorn berries are tender and beginning to fall apart, taste and add salt and pepper as desired. To serve, finish with a sprinkle of chopped basil or dollop of pesto and the shredded Parmesan.

(Ein)Corn Chowder

Corn chowder is an all-season dish thanks to frozen corn, but if you have a bounty of fresh corn in season, it's a must—both summery and hearty. A little einkorn flour provides the soup with that chowdery thickness; for an extra-creamy chowder, blend half of the finished chowder in a blender or food processor and add it back to the soup for serving.

MAKES 4 TO 6 SERVINGS

3 tablespoons unsalted butter
1 medium white onion, diced
1 teaspoon kosher salt
1 medium stalk celery, diced
1 (4-ounce) jar diced pimentos, drained
Kernels from 8 ears sweet corn, or 6 cups frozen corn

3 cloves garlic, minced
2 tablespoons whole grain einkorn flour
3 cups vegetable broth
½ cup heavy cream
3 green onions, green parts only, cut into slivers

1   In a large saucepan or Dutch oven, melt the butter over medium heat. Add the onion and salt and cook over medium heat until the onion starts to look translucent, about 5 minutes. Add the celery, pimentos, and corn and cook for 10 minutes until they start to soften. Add the garlic and cook for another minute or so, until fragrant. Add the einkorn flour, stirring well until it mixes in and coats everything. Add the broth and bring to a boil. As soon as it reaches a rolling boil, cover the pot and turn the heat down to medium-low. Simmer for 20 minutes to let the soup come together.

2   Uncover the pot and check that the vegetables are cooked to your liking; add a few minutes to the cooking time if needed.

3   If you like a creamier soup, blend about a cup of the soup for 30 seconds or so, until smooth, then add it back to the pot and bring it back to a simmer. Stir in the cream and serve garnished with green onions.

Slow-Cooker Chamim Beef Stew

We do a family Shabbat dinner on Friday nights, and I'm often teaching that day. This traditional Shabbat stew comes to the rescue! The stew was designed to throw everything in a pot for twenty-five hours so nobody has to cook on the day of rest. It might sound a little strange to add whole unpeeled eggs to a stew, but this is how chamim (also called cholent) is traditionally made. Trust me, when you pull them out and peel them, you'll find they have absorbed qualities from the stew, which makes them a great accompaniment to bites of the stew. I like to serve them separately, so I put them in a bowl alongside a little grainy mustard and let people peel and dip as they see fit.

MAKES 8 TO 10 SERVINGS

2 medium yellow onions, diced
Peeled cloves from 1 whole head
   of garlic
1½ pounds red potatoes, quartered
3 pounds chuck roast, cubed
1 cup einkorn berries
½ cup dried chickpeas
1 tablespoon sweet paprika

1 tablespoon kosher salt
2 teaspoons ground cumin
Freshly ground black pepper
2 quarts low-sodium beef broth
1 tablespoon honey or silan
   (date syrup)
4 to 8 eggs (optional)

1   In a large slow cooker or a large ovenproof pot, layer the onions and the garlic cloves. Add the quartered potatoes in a layer, then the cubed meat. Scatter the einkorn berries and chickpeas over everything, then sprinkle over the paprika, salt, cumin, and black pepper. Pour the broth over everything and make sure it's all submerged. If needed, add a little water to just cover the ingredients. Add the honey. Finally, rinse the eggs well and nestle them into the broth.

2   Set the slow cooker on low for 8 to 12 hours or, to cook in the oven, set the oven to 250 degrees F and cook, covered, for about 12 hours.

3   To serve, pull the eggs out and rinse them, then place them in a bowl to pass at the table so people can eat them as they like.

Mains

Cheesy Broccoli Bake

This is an einkorn take on mac 'n' cheese with some added broccoli: comfort food at its finest. If you have time, toast the einkorn berries for a richer flavor, but I've skipped this step plenty of times and it's still very satisfying. You can prepare this dish in advance and keep it in the fridge overnight (see Note).

MAKES 6 TO 8 SERVINGS

2 tablespoons extra-virgin olive oil, plus more for the pan
1 cup einkorn berries
1 large head of broccoli (1½ to 2 pounds)
1½ teaspoons kosher salt, plus more as needed
Freshly ground black pepper
1½ cups (6 ounces) shredded cheddar cheese

1 cup (4 ounces) shredded Gruyère
1½ cups heavy cream
1 cup whole milk
3 eggs
½ cup coarsely chopped parsley
2 cloves garlic, minced
1 medium shallot, minced
1 tablespoon grainy mustard

1   Preheat the oven to 400 degrees F. Prepare a 9-by-13-inch baking pan or equivalent oval gratin dish by brushing with a bit of olive oil.

2   Put the einkorn berries on a rimmed baking sheet and roast in the oven for 15 to 20 minutes, until a toasty aroma starts to fill the kitchen.

3   Meanwhile, cut the broccoli into small florets. Peel the stalk and cut it into small disks about the same size as the florets. Put all the broccoli in a medium bowl, add the 2 tablespoons olive oil, and toss to coat well, then season with a bit of salt and pepper.

4   Transfer the toasted einkorn to a small bowl and put the broccoli on the same baking sheet. Roast for about 20 minutes, until it's soft on the inside and just starting to crisp at the edges. Set aside. Lower the oven temperature to 350 degrees F for the final bake.

5   While the broccoli is roasting, bring a medium pot of water to a boil. Add the toasted einkorn berries and cook them for 25 minutes, until tender and some of the grains are starting to swell and break open. Drain and set aside to cool a bit.

$\longrightarrow$

6   In a large bowl, mix the cheddar and Gruyère together and set aside 1 cup of the mixture for the topping. Add the cream, milk, eggs, parsley, garlic, shallot, mustard, and the 1½ teaspoons salt to the bowl with the cheese. Season with pepper and beat until no egg yolk is visible. Fold the einkorn berries and broccoli into the cheese mixture, then tumble it into the prepared baking pan and smooth it out so everything is submerged in the liquid.

7   Top with the reserved cup of cheese, cover the pan tightly with foil, and bake for 25 minutes. Remove the foil and turn the heat to broil. Broil for 5 to 10 minutes, until the top is golden brown. Check on it starting at 5 minutes to make sure it doesn't burn. Serve while it's still bubbling hot.

NOTE: If you want to prepare the dish the day before you bake it, put it in the refrigerator after you've covered it with foil. When you're ready to bake, preheat the oven to 350 degrees F and bake for 30 to 35 minutes and broil 5 to 10 minutes to finish.

Japanese Curry Pot Pie

A few years ago, I helped a friend with a project wherein he made the most delicious Japanese curry dish—and he also made, separately, a pot pie. This inspired me to marry the two in a curried pot pie, and I have to say the result is pretty satisfying. Japanese curry mix is full of umami; my favorite brand is Golden Curry, which is widely available in heat levels from mild to extra spicy, but other Japanese curry mixes will work here too.

MAKES 6 TO 8 SERVINGS

For the dough
1 cup (120 grams) whole grain
  einkorn flour
¼ teaspoon kosher salt
¼ teaspoon sugar
6 tablespoons (¾ stick) cold
  unsalted butter
3 to 4 tablespoons ice water

For the filling
2 tablespoons unsalted butter
1 tablespoon sunflower oil or other
  neutral oil

1½ pounds boneless, skinless chicken
  breast, cut into cubes
1 medium white onion, diced
2 large carrots, cut into
  ½-inch-thick slices
8 ounces button mushrooms, cut into
  ½-inch-thick slices
1 pound yellow potatoes, cubed
3½ cups water
1 (3.2-ounce) box Japanese curry
  mix, such as Golden Curry
½ cup frozen peas

1   To make the dough, in a large bowl, combine the flour, salt, and sugar. Cut the cold butter into pieces and put one-quarter of it back in the fridge to keep cold. Using a pastry cutter, cut up and mix the rest of the butter pieces into the flour mixture until it looks a little shaggy. Take the rest of the cold butter pieces out of the fridge and cut them in until most of the dough looks sandy, but some larger butter pieces remain. Add the ice water 1 tablespoon at a time, mixing with the cutter, until it all comes together. Turn the dough out onto a clean work surface and knead one or two times, then press it into a disk. Wrap in plastic wrap and refrigerate at least 1 hour and up to 3 days.

$\longrightarrow$

2   To make the filling, set a large, lidded pot over medium heat and melt the butter until foaming. Add the oil and swirl it into the butter, then add the chicken and sauté until the cubes start to brown, turning them occasionally, about 5 minutes. Add the onion and sauté for 5 minutes, until fragrant but not browned. Add the carrots, mushrooms, and potatoes and stir, then add the water. Cover and cook for 20 minutes, until the vegetables are tender. Add the curry mix and decrease the heat to medium-low. Simmer, uncovered, for 10 more minutes.

3   Preheat the oven to 375 degrees F. Retrieve the dough from the fridge and roll it out to about 9½ by 13½ inches. Pour the vegetables into a 9-by-13-inch baking dish. Even out the surface and place the dough atop the curry. Tuck the edges of the dough in against the side of the dish to completely cover the curry. Cut three slits in the top of the dough to allow steam to vent. Bake, uncovered, for 35 to 40 minutes, until the filling is bubbling hot and the crust is golden. Let the pie cool and set just a bi, or serve it right out of the oven, scooping big servings of curry with a bit of crust into bowls.

Hearty Harvest Bowls
with Balsamic Brussels Sprouts and Butternut Squash

With einkorn, lentils, and plenty of colorful winter vegetables, these bowls are a deeply satisfying all-in-one dinner. The brussels sprouts and squash look like jewels, and when you add the beets to the serving bowls, the colors are as pleasing as the flavors.

Makes 4 to 6 servings

½ cup extra-virgin olive oil
¼ cup balsamic vinegar
2 tablespoons Dijon mustard
2 tablespoons honey
4 cloves garlic, minced
1 teaspoon kosher salt
Freshly ground black pepper
1½ pounds brussels sprouts,
   cut into quarters

1 small butternut squash, peeled,
   seeded, and cubed
1½ cups einkorn berries
½ cup brown lentils
8 ounces pickled or roasted beets,
   cut into small cubes (optional)
Leaves from 1 small sprig of rosemary,
   minced fine

1   Preheat the oven to 425 degrees F.

2   In a small bowl, whisk together the olive oil, balsamic vinegar, mustard, honey, garlic, salt, and pepper to taste. Put the brussels sprouts and butternut squash in a medium bowl and pour half of the marinade over the vegetables. Transfer the vegetables to a rimmed baking sheet and set it on the middle rack of the oven for 30 to 40 minutes (depending on how crispy you like them).

3   Meanwhile, bring a large pot of water to a boil. Add the einkorn and lentils and cook over medium-high heat, uncovered, for 25 minutes or until tender. Drain and return the einkorn and lentils to the pot; cover to keep warm while the vegetables finish cooking.

4   Transfer the einkorn and lentils to one large serving bowl or divide among 4 to 6 smaller bowls. Top with brussels sprouts and squash, then add the beets. Drizzle with some of the reserved balsamic dressing and add a sprinkle of rosemary.

Cilantro-Lime Grain Bowls

with Roasted Summer Vegetables

I love tomatoes, and I wait for the season like a true fanatic. When tomatoes, zucchini, and corn are in season, this dish highlights all the bright and festive flavors of summer; or you can bring summer into any season with these easy-to-find ingredients. This is a refreshing summer dinner on its own, but if you want to add protein, stir in a drained can of chickpeas or some shredded rotisserie chicken.

MAKES 4 TO 6 SERVINGS

1 tablespoon plus 1 teaspoon
   kosher salt
3 ears of corn, shucked, or 2 cups
   frozen corn
2 cups einkorn
3 tablespoons extra-virgin olive
   oil, divided

Zest and juice of 1 medium lime
2 pints cherry tomatoes
2 medium zucchini, cut into
   ½-inch pieces
2 cloves garlic, minced
Freshly ground black pepper
½ cup cilantro leaves

1   Preheat the oven to 450 degrees F.

2   If you are using fresh corn, put a large pot of water on to boil and add
    1 tablespoon of the salt. The water should taste salty, like seawater. Boil the ears
    of corn for about 3 minutes, then remove and set aside to cool before cutting
    the kernels from the cobs.

3   Add the einkorn to the same pot of water and boil, uncovered, for 25 minutes.
    Make sure the level of water always covers the grain; if you need to add a bit
    more water to cover, just bring it back to a quick boil. If you're using frozen corn,
    add the kernels for the last 3 minutes of cooking. Drain and return to the pot. If
    you're using fresh corn, add the kernels now. Add 1 tablespoon of the olive oil to
    the einkorn, along with the lime zest and juice, and stir.

4   In a medium bowl, combine the cherry tomatoes, zucchini, and garlic with the
    remaining 2 tablespoons olive oil and remaining 1 teaspoon salt. Spread the
    vegetables evenly on a baking sheet and bake for about 15 minutes, until slightly
    charred and fragrant.

5   Fold the roasted vegetables gently into the einkorn. Garnish with the fresh
    cilantro leaves and serve immediately.

Dill and Lemon Pilaf
with Simple Roasted Fish

I love having fish dishes in my repertoire because they're so quick to make. This is a perfect example: Once you get your pilaf going and the fish in the oven, everything can be on the table in half an hour.

MAKES 4 SERVINGS

2 tablespoons unsalted butter

½ medium yellow onion, diced

1 cup einkorn berries

1¾ cups vegetable broth or chicken broth

2 medium lemons

4 (6- to 8-ounce) cod fillets

2 tablespoons extra-virgin olive oil, divided

1 teaspoon kosher salt

¼ teaspoon freshly ground white or black pepper

2 tablespoons chopped fresh dill, plus more for serving

1   In a medium saucepan over medium-high heat, melt the butter. When it starts to sizzle, add the onion and stir until it starts to get soft and slightly translucent, about 4 minutes. Add the einkorn berries and stir for 1 minute, until the berries are nicely coated with butter and the onion is mixed in. Add the broth, bring to a boil, then cover and decrease the heat to medium-low. Simmer, undisturbed, for 35 minutes.

2   Meanwhile, preheat the oven to 450 degrees F. Zest and juice one of the lemons and thinly slice four rounds from the other; set aside.

3   Check the einkorn to see whether the liquid is totally absorbed and some of the grains have started to split open. If not, let it cook, uncovered, until the liquid is mostly evaporated. Remove from the heat, put a clean kitchen towel over the top, and replace the lid. Let rest for about 10 minutes.

4   Put the fish fillets in an oven-safe dish and brush with half of the olive oil. Season with the salt and pepper and layer a slice of lemon on each fillet. Brush the lemon with a bit more olive oil. Roast for 10 to 15 minutes, until the fish is cooked and the lemon has started to caramelize.

5   To finish the pilaf, fluff the einkorn with a fork and add the lemon zest and juice and dill. Stir to mix well. Divide among 4 plates and top with a serving of fish and a little more fresh dill. Alternatively, serve the pilaf and fish in one big dish, family style.

One-Pot French Onion Casserole

Who doesn't like the melty comfort of French onion soup? This recipe combines elements of the bistro classic with American comfort food in a casserole fortified with einkorn berries and a touch of einkorn flour. It's great on a cold day! A dampened crumpled sheet of parchment paper placed atop the casserole keeps everything moist as it bakes.

MAKES 6 TO 8 SERVINGS

2 tablespoons unsalted butter

2 large yellow onions, sliced

1½ teaspoons kosher salt, divided

4 medium boneless, skinless chicken breasts (about 1½ lbs) cut into 1-inch cubes

2 cups einkorn berries

2 tablespoons whole grain einkorn flour

2 teaspoons fresh thyme leaves

½ cup sherry or white wine

4 cups chicken, beef, or vegetable broth

1 cup (4 ounces) shredded Gruyère cheese

1   Preheat the oven to 350 degrees F.

2   In a large ovenproof pot over medium heat, melt the butter until it's just starting to bubble. Add the onions and ½ teaspoon of the salt and cook, stirring occasionally, for about 10 minutes, until the onions start to become amber in color. Push them to the sides of the pot and raise the temperature to high. Put the chicken pieces in the middle of the pot and sprinkle with the remaining 1 teaspoon salt. Cook without stirring for about 5 minutes to let some of the pieces brown. Add the einkorn berries, flour, and thyme leaves and stir everything until it's well combined. Add the sherry and, as it heats, use a wooden spoon to scrape any bits off the bottom of the pot. Pour the broth over everything, stir to combine, and bring to a boil. If you have parchment paper, wet and crumple up a piece and set it directly on the food in the pot (or skip this detail). Cover the pot with the lid and transfer to the oven to bake for 1 hour.

3   Remove the pot from the oven and take the lid off. Discard the parchment paper and sprinkle the shredded cheese on top. Set the oven to broil and slide the pot under the broiler for about 5 minutes, until the top of the casserole has a golden-brown cheesy crust. Since all broilers are a bit different, check the casserole's progress once or twice. Serve hot directly from the pot.

Southern Chicken and Dumplings

I learned this dish from my mother-in-law. She learned it by making it with her grandmother time and time again; it was never written down, so I learned it the same way. The whole grain einkorn dumplings add heartiness to a simple, rustic bowl of goodness.

MAKES 4 TO 6 SERVINGS

2 medium boneless, skinless chicken
    breasts, about ½ pound
8½ cups water, divided
½ teaspoon kosher salt
1 tablespoon bouillon paste or
    1 bouillon cube
1 egg

¼ cup buttermilk
2½ cups whole grain einkorn flour,
    divided, plus more for dusting
Freshly ground black pepper
A handful of fresh sage leaves,
    cut into slivers, or ¼ teaspoon
    dried sage

1   Put the chicken breasts in a large pot or Dutch oven and cover with 8 cups of the water. Bring to a boil over high heat, then lower the heat to maintain a simmer and cook, uncovered, for 20 minutes, skimming any foam that rises to the surface. Remove the chicken to a plate. Return the liquid to a simmer and add the bouillon to the pot, keeping the liquid simmering.

2   In a medium bowl, whisk the egg and buttermilk to combine, then whisk in the remaining ½ cup water. Add 2 cups of the flour ½ cup at time, stirring to form a dough. Spread the last ½ cup flour on a clean work surface and turn the dough out onto it. Knead to incorporate as much flour as you can.

3   Gather the dough into a ball and cut it into four equal pieces. Cut each quarter of the dough into four pieces and, with your hands, roll each one out into a rope about 8 inches long and transfer each to the simmering broth as you work. Keep flouring the surface as needed (it's okay if plenty of loose flour makes its way into the broth, thickening it). As the pot gets crowded with dumplings, push them to the sides of the pot to make room in the middle for the new ones. When all sixteen pieces are in the broth, shred the chicken breasts and add to the pot. Grind in a generous amount of black pepper, stir, and finish with the sage. Serve hot in big soup bowls.

Bean and Cheese Burritos

Burritos are some of the world's most beloved grab-and-go meals. And though they're found on many a fast-food menu, at heart they are far from junk food. For a healthy and delicious take on the burrito, look no farther than this recipe. You can make these ahead for an easy lunch on a busy day.

MAKES 4 BURRITOS

2 cups dried pinto beans

3 cloves garlic, peeled

1¼ teaspoons kosher salt, divided, plus more to taste

2 tablespoons extra-virgin olive oil

1 medium yellow onion, finely chopped

¼ teaspoon ground cumin

¼ teaspoon dried oregano

4 Tender Tortillas (page 113) or store-bought

1½ cups (6 ounces) shredded cheddar or Mexican blend cheese

Guacamole, salsa verde, and/or sour cream, for serving (optional)

1   Rinse the beans and pick through them to make sure there are no small rocks. Put them in a medium bowl and cover with water; soak for at least 4 hours or overnight.

2   Drain the beans and put them in a large pot along with the garlic cloves. Cover the beans with fresh water by about an inch. Bring to a boil. Decrease the heat to low, skim any foam from the top of the water, and simmer until the beans are fully cooked, usually about an hour. After 30 minutes, add 1 teaspoon of the salt. If you need to add water to make sure the beans stay covered as they cook, add just enough to keep them covered. Test for doneness by fishing out a bean and biting it; if it's soft all the way through, they're about done. Mash them a bit and keep them simmering while you cook the onion.

3   In a large pan over medium-high heat, heat the olive oil until it's shimmering a bit. Add the onion and the remaining ¼ teaspoon salt. Cook, stirring often, for about 5 minutes, until the onion starts to look golden and smell sweet. Add the cumin and oregano and cook for 30 seconds more. When the beans have very little liquid left and they're smashed and becoming mushy, add them to the onion mixture and cook until it has a thick, slightly velvety texture suitable for filling burritos.

4   Warm the tortillas. To fill the burritos, place ¾ to 1 cup of bean mixture in a horizontal line across the center of each tortilla, leaving an inch or two at the edge of the tortilla. Top each with one-quarter of the cheese.

5   To roll each burrito, fold two edges of the tortilla over the filling (these will be the top and bottom), then fold one side over the beans. With both hands, roll the burrito up so that the filling is snugly enclosed in the tortilla; keep it seam side down so it stays tightly rolled.

6   Transfer the burritos to serving plates and eat them just like this, hot and freshly rolled, with your chosen accompaniments. Or, to get the cheese really melty before serving, heat a large pan over medium heat and cook the burritos seam side down for 2 minutes before serving. You can also let them cool and wrap each snugly in parchment paper and refrigerate for up to 3 days.

Bibimbap-ish Einkorn

Any chance I get to eat a dish with crispy grains, I'm in. That's why I love dolsot bibimbap, a Korean protein-and-veggie bowl built on a layer of crispy rice. I like to use teriyaki or miso-flavored baked tofu for an easy, flavorful addition without the extra work of marinating. This is my einkorn version of bibimbap, simplified for a weeknight, giving me a one-pan dish full of flavor (and that crispiness too).

MAKES 4 TO 6 SERVINGS

1 cup einkorn berries
2 tablespoons sunflower oil or other neutral oil
8 ounces fresh shiitake mushrooms, larger ones halved
¼ cup soy sauce
2 tablespoons mirin

¼ teaspoon kosher salt
1 pound fresh spinach
1 medium carrot, shredded
1 small zucchini, shredded
1 cup kimchi (optional)
1 (7-ounce) block baked firm tofu, cubed

1   Put the einkorn berries in a large pot and cover with water by about 2 inches. Bring to a boil over high heat and let the einkorn cook, uncovered, for about 25 minutes. If the water looks like it might boil over, lower the heat to keep a rolling boil going without boiling over. If at any point the einkorn isn't totally underwater, add a bit more water to cover. The berries are done when they are plump and popping open a little. Drain and set aside.

2   In a large pan (at least 12 inches) with a lid, heat the oil over medium-high heat until shimmering. Add the mushrooms and spread them out in an even layer. Let them cook undisturbed for about 5 minutes so they brown a bit. Add the soy sauce, mirin, and salt and scrape with a wooden spoon to loosen any mushrooms stuck to the pan. Add the spinach and a splash of water and cover the pan to wilt the spinach.(If all the spinach doesn't fit at first, add it in batches, letting it wilt for about 3 minutes before you add more.) When the spinach is wilted, about 3 minutes, add the shredded carrot and zucchini and stir to mix. Cook for another 5 to 10 minutes until the carrot is no longer raw but still has a bit of snap.

3   Stir in the cooked einkorn, then press the mixture down in the pan and leave it on the heat for another 3 minutes to form a crust on the bottom. To serve, spoon into bowls and top with kimchi and tofu.

Spring Vegetable Risotto

Delicate spring vegetables like asparagus and peas pair well with the soft texture of a risotto; if you happen to have an abundance of fresh young vegetables on hand, use them here. Using a blender or food processor to crack grains before cooking allows more starch to release when the grain is cooking, making for a creamier dish. Note that you may not need to use all the liquid in the dish, and that's okay. You want to have enough hot broth on hand to get the risotto to the right consistency; store any that's left over for another use.

MAKES 4 TO 6 SERVINGS

4 cups chicken or vegetable broth
4 cups water
1 bunch asparagus, trimmed and cut into 1-inch pieces
2 cups einkorn berries
2 tablespoons extra-virgin olive oil
2 tablespoons unsalted butter, divided
1 small white onion, chopped fine

Kosher salt and freshly ground black pepper
½ cup dry white wine
1 cup shelled peas, fresh or thawed from frozen
½ cup (1½ ounces) finely ground or shredded Parmesan cheese
2 red radishes, sliced thin
2 green onions, green parts only, sliced thin

1   In a large saucepan, combine the broth and water and bring to a boil over high heat. Lower the heat to medium and add the asparagus. Simmer for 5 minutes, then scoop the asparagus out with a slotted spoon and transfer to a plate lined with paper towels. Cover the pot and turn the heat down to low to keep the broth at a simmer.

2   In a blender or food processor, pulse the einkorn three or four times until it looks like coarse sand with a few bigger pieces. Don't overdo it, just take it from whole berries to cracked grain.

3   In a large pan or Dutch oven over medium-high heat, heat the olive oil and 1 tablespoon of the butter until the butter melts. Add the onion and cook, stirring, for about 5 minutes, until it starts to look translucent. Season with salt and pepper.

4   Add the cracked einkorn and stir to coat with oil. Let it cook for about
    3 minutes, stirring a bit, until the grain starts to smell a bit toasty (it won't
    look any browner). Add the wine, which will hiss a little, suggesting the
    grain is nice and hot and will absorb the liquid. When the wine is almost
    completely absorbed, about 5 minutes, add half of the broth and use a
    wooden spoon to scrape up any bits at the bottom of the pan.

5   Cover the pot and reduce the heat to medium-low. Simmer for 10 minutes
    without lifting the lid. Uncover the pot, add 2 ladlefuls of broth, and stir to
    loosen any grain from the bottom.

6   Cover the pot and cook, undisturbed, for 10 more minutes. Remove the lid
    and raise the heat back to medium-high. Stir in about 2 cups more broth a
    ladleful at a time, stirring between additions, and scrape the bottom of the
    pot to loosen any stuck grain. Taste the einkorn: When it's done, it will be
    soft but still a little al dente. The texture of the risotto should be thick but
    still loose enough to ladle into bowls. If it's too thick, stir in a bit more broth;
    if it's too thin, raise the heat and stir for a minute or two to allow some liquid
    to evaporate.

7   Stir in the cooked asparagus, peas, the remaining 1 tablespoon butter, and
    Parmesan cheese. Taste and adjust the salt and pepper as needed. Ladle
    into bowls and garnish with the sliced radishes and green onions.

Cheese-to-the-Edges Pan Pizza

Detroit-style pizza is rectangular deep-dish pizza with a thick, airy, bready crust and a cheese layer that goes to the edges of the pie. Contact with the pan sides gives the cheese layer its own crispy crustiness. I use a metal pan (the preferred pan for Detroit-style pizza), but I also tested it with a 9-by-13-inch baking dish, and it worked great.

MAKES ONE 9-BY-13-INCH PAN PIZZA

2¼ cups (270 grams) whole grain einkorn flour

1½ teaspoons kosher salt, plus more as needed

¾ teaspoon instant yeast

¾ cup water

2 tablespoons extra-virgin olive oil

1 (14.5-ounce) can diced tomatoes

1 small clove garlic, minced

½ teaspoon dried oregano

3 cups (12 ounces) shredded mozzarella cheese

1 tablespoon Parmesan cheese

Pizza toppings of your choice (optional)

Torn fresh basil leaves, for garnish

1   In a large mixing bowl, stir together the flour, salt, and yeast. Drizzle in the water and mix until a dough forms. Shape the dough gently into a ball and let it rest in the bowl for 20 minutes, lightly covered with a dish towel. Knead the dough by folding it up and over itself in the bowl, then turn the bowl a quarter turn and fold again; repeat these steps so that you've turned the bowl all the way around once and folded it four times. Let it rest another 20 minutes, by which time it should be looking a little bigger. Do another round of folding the dough in the bowl, then let it rest for 20 more minutes.

2   Drizzle the oil over the bottom of a deep 9-by-13-inch rectangular baking pan. Put the dough in the pan and start to stretch it out toward the edges. Flip the dough over once to get oil on both sides, then keep stretching it toward the edges. If it doesn't reach the edges, let it rest for 10 minutes, then keep stretching it. Cover with a kitchen towel and let it rest at room temperature for 1 hour.

3   Preheat the oven to 450 degrees F.

4   To make the sauce, put the tomatoes, garlic, and oregano in a blender. If the tomatoes don't already contain salt, add about ¼ teaspoon. Blend until smooth.

5   Slide the pan into the oven to parbake the dough for 6 minutes; it will start to look a little lacquered on top. Remove the pan from the oven and pour the sauce over the dough. Spread the sauce out evenly, then sprinkle the cheese over the pizza in an even layer, making sure the cheese comes right up to the edges of the pan. Add toppings if you're using them.

6   Bake for 12 to 15 minutes, until the cheese is bubbly and browned a bit on top. Pull the pizza from the oven and run a knife around the edges of the pan to ensure the crispy cheese border stays attached to the pizza rather than the pan when you dish out slices. Top the pizza with torn basil leaves, slice it, and serve it right from the pan like 1970s moms did. Or, if you prefer to slice it on a cutting board, it should slide right out.

Classic Pasta Marinara
with Meatballs

There is nothing more comforting to me than a bowl of hot pasta with meatballs and tomato sauce. Making your own einkorn pasta from scratch can be a fun project when you have time (see recipe following this one), but there are great einkorn pastas on the market too. Grab a box if you aren't inclined to go all-in with scratch-cooking this dish.

MAKES 4 TO 6 SERVINGS

For the meatballs
Extra-virgin olive oil, for greasing
   the pan
1 slice stale einkorn bread (page 93) or
   pita (page 103), torn into pieces
2 pounds ground beef
2 eggs
¼ cup chicken broth
1 large shallot, diced
2 cloves garlic, minced
1 tablespoon plus 2 teaspoons kosher
   salt, divided, plus more as needed
1 tablespoon nutritional yeast
   (optional)
1 teaspoon sweet paprika
1 teaspoon mustard powder
¼ teaspoon freshly ground
   black pepper

For the sauce
2 (28-ounce) cans whole
   peeled tomatoes
2 tablespoons extra-virgin olive oil
1 medium yellow onion, diced
1 medium carrot, shredded
4 cloves garlic, minced
½ teaspoon red pepper flakes
1 teaspoon dried oregano

For assembly
1 pound fresh einkorn fettuccine
   (recipe follows) or dried store-
   bought einkorn pasta
Handful of fresh basil leaves, torn

1   To make the meatballs, preheat the oven to 400 degrees F. Oil a baking sheet with olive oil and set aside.

2   Put the stale bread in a blender or food processor and pulse to make coarse bread crumbs.

3   In a large bowl, combine the ground beef, eggs, broth, shallot, garlic, 1 tablespoon of the salt, nutritional yeast, paprika, mustard powder, and black pepper. Add the bread crumbs and mix well until all the ingredients are evenly distributed.

4   Scoop out about ¼ cup of the meatball mixture, roll it into a ball between your palms, and place it on the prepared baking sheet. Continue until you have about twenty meatballs, which should all fit on one baking sheet; if you have a few more, it's fine to crowd them a bit (just don't pack them tight). Bake for 15 to 20 minutes, or until browned all the way through.

5   Meanwhile, make the sauce: Empty both cans of tomatoes into a large bowl and squeeze the tomatoes with your hands to break them up so they have the consistency of a chunky sauce. Scoop 1 cup into a small bowl and set both bowls aside.

6   In a large pot or Dutch oven, heat the olive oil over medium heat until shimmering. Add the onion and shredded carrot and cook for about 10 minutes, stirring occasionally so they cook evenly. Stir in the minced garlic, red pepper flakes, oregano, and the remaining 2 teaspoons salt. Add the large bowl of tomatoes to the onion mixture, stirring and scraping the bottom of the pot to loosen anything that might be getting stuck. Cover the pot, lower the heat to medium-low, and simmer for an hour.

7   To assemble the dish, bring a large pot of salted water to a boil over high heat. Drop the fresh pasta into the water and cook for 1 to 2 minutes. When the noodles all float to the top, they're done. If you're using dried pasta, follow the cooking instructions on the package.

8   While the pasta water is coming to a boil, add the cooked meatballs (and any juices that have accumulated in the pan) to the simmering pot of sauce; cook for 10 minutes. Stir in the reserved cup of hand-crushed tomatoes. Taste and add salt as needed.

9   Drain the cooked pasta, divide it among serving plates, top with sauce, and serve immediately, scattered with torn fresh basil leaves.

Fresh Einkorn Fettuccine

Making homemade pasta is a project for when you have some leisure time. If you haven't don't it before, I urge you to try it at least once: There's something magical and meditative about it. You will need a pasta machine for this recipe. I use a hand-cranked Atlas pasta machine; if you have a different one, follow the manufacturer's instructions for rolling out and cutting the dough. Though the instructions here are for making fettuccine noodles, this dough can be shaped into any pasta style you like. If your dough isn't turning out smooth, try adding an additional egg yolk. Since the eggs will need to be at room temperature for this recipe, take them out of the fridge at least 30 minutes before you'll need them.

MAKES 4 SERVINGS

4 cups whole grain einkorn flour
1 tablespoon kosher salt

4 eggs, at room temperature

1   Scoop the flour and salt into a pile on a clean work surface. In the center, make a well that's deep enough to hold the eggs. Crack the eggs into the well and use a fork to gently break open the yolks. Start beating a bit of the flour into the eggs a little at a time with the fork until the eggs are fully incorporated and a sticky dough has formed.

2   Knead the dough for about 10 minutes, adding more of the flour and kneading it in until incorporated (resist the urge to add too much flour at once). Gradually, the dough will transform from a sticky mass into a smooth, supple, cohesive ball of dough. Cover the dough and let it rest at room temperature for about an hour.

3   To make the pasta noodles, set a pasta machine to its widest setting and lay out several clean kitchen towels on a work surface. Cut the dough into four equal pieces and pat each piece into a rough rectangle shape. Run the first piece through the widest setting on the machine. Fold it in thirds (like a letter) and run it through again. Rest it on the kitchen towels and run the other three pieces through the machine in the same way. When you lay them on the towels to rest, ensure they don't overlap.

$\longrightarrow$

4 Adjust the machine's width down by one number and run the dough through again, starting with the first piece you made. Continue the process of thinning the dough until it's at your desired thickness. For fettuccine, I usually take it down to the "6" setting on my Atlas machine. Your machine's instructions will guide you, and with a bit of experimenting, you'll figure out what works best. With each step, spread the dough sheets out on the clean towels, not letting them touch.

5 This slow thinning of the dough develops the pasta's structure. If a dough sheet tears or has a flaw you want to fix, open the machine to a wider setting and do the letter-fold thing again, then go down one setting at a time until you get to the desired thinness.

6 Let the sheets rest on the kitchen towels for about 10 minutes to further dry them out before cutting. When the dough is almost at the point of feeling leathery, it's ready to cut.

7 Use your pasta machine's attachment to cut the dough into the desired shape. Once cut, hang the noodles to dry on a rack (or the back of a chair) for 15 minutes. Cook fresh pasta within 30 minutes of drying it or store it in the fridge tightly wrapped in parchment paper and plastic wrap.

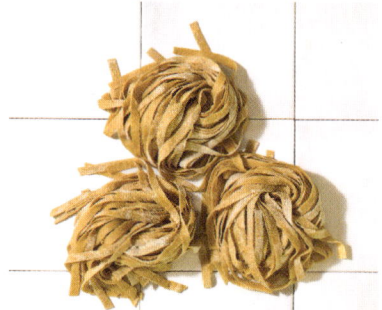

Grilled Cheese Sandwiches
with Easy Tomato Dipping Sauce

These grilled cheese sandwiches are one of my go-to easy dinners. If you'd prefer to serve them with soup rather than a dipping sauce, try the Tomato Bread Soup on page 45. I also like them with a little store-bought pesto for a twist.

MAKES 4 SANDWICHES

For the dipping sauce
3 cloves garlic, sliced
¼ cup extra-virgin olive oil
1 (6-ounce) can tomato paste
Pinch of red pepper flakes
Leaves from 3 sprigs fresh
   thyme (optional)
Warm water, for thinning the sauce
¼ teaspoon sugar, plus more to taste
Kosher salt and freshly ground
   black pepper

For the sandwiches
8 slices Everyday Einkorn Sandwich
   Bread (page 93) or store-bought
¼ cup (½ stick) unsalted
   butter, softened
4 slices Gruyère cheese
4 slices sharp cheddar cheese

1   Preheat the oven to 325 degrees F.

2   To make the dipping sauce, in a small saucepan over medium heat, warm the olive oil and garlic slices. As the oil slowly heats, the garlic slices will take on an amber hue in about 5 minutes. Remove the garlic to a plate and add the can of tomato paste to the pan. Stir to warm the tomato paste, about 3 minutes (it will still look like tomato paste floating in oil). Add the red pepper flakes and thyme to the oil and fill the tomato paste can with warm water. Slowly add the water, stirring constantly, until the sauce looks smooth. Add the sugar and season with salt and pepper. Taste and add a bit more salt or sugar as needed. Turn the heat down to its lowest setting to keep warm while you prepare the sandwiches.

$\longrightarrow$

3 To make the sandwiches, butter one side of each slice of bread and set 4 of them buttered side down in a large sauté pan. Layer each slice of bread with 1 slice of Gruyère and 1 slice of cheddar. Put the pan over medium heat and toast, until the cheese is starting to melt. Put the second slice of bread on each sandwich, buttered side facing up. Turn the sandwiches and toast on the second side. If the first side of any of the sandwiches doesn't have a nice golden color, turn them again. At this point, the cheese will be melted enough that the sandwich will stay together when flipping, so keep turning and toasting both sides until the color is just as you like it.

4 Remove the sandwiches to plates and cut them in half. Divide the warm sauce into little ramekins for dipping or serve it in one bowl with a spoon for everyone to serve themselves. If you like, mince up the cooked garlic you removed from the oil and sprinkle it on top of the sauce for a little flourish.

Oven Shawarma
with Pita

This is one of my family's all-time favorite dinners. I usually serve it with a very simple cabbage salad and a little tahini for drizzling. If you have time, it's best to marinate the chicken for up to a day before cooking it, but at minimum, an hour will do.

MAKES 4 TO 6 SERVINGS

3 pounds boneless, skinless
   chicken thighs
1 large red onion, sliced thick
Juice of 2 medium lemons
½ cup extra-virgin olive oil
6 cloves garlic, minced
1 tablespoon sweet paprika
2½ teaspoons ground cumin
1½ teaspoons kosher salt

¾ teaspoon ground turmeric
¼ teaspoon ground coriander
¼ teaspoon ground cinnamon
Pinch of freshly ground black pepper
1 batch Versatile Pita Bread
   (page 103)
Thinly sliced cabbage, for serving
Tahini, for serving

1   Put the chicken thighs and onion slices in a large container with a lid. In a small bowl, combine the lemon juice, olive oil, garlic, paprika, cumin, salt, turmeric, coriander, cinnamon, and pepper; stir to mix. Pour over the chicken and onion and toss to coat. Cover the container and let the chicken marinate in the fridge for at least 1 hour and up to 1 day.

2   Take the chicken out of the refrigerator to let it come to room temperature. Preheat the oven to 450 degrees F. Spread the chicken and onion on a baking sheet and roast for 45 to 60 minutes, until the chicken is cooked through and the onion slices are charred in places. Let the chicken and onion cool a bit on the pan, then transfer to a cutting board to chop them into bite-size pieces. Stuff each pita with the shawarma and top with cabbage and a drizzle of tahini.

Stuffed Eggplant Parmesan

Eggplant Parmesan was one of my favorite meals when I was kid, and when I grew up I was very disappointed to learn how much effort it takes to make. Not this version, though! While the eggplant halves roast, the filling comes together. The eggplant halves are easy to stuff and bake in the oven with a melty layer of mozzarella.

MAKES 4 TO 8 SERVINGS

4 small to medium eggplants
 (8 to 10 ounces each)
3 tablespoons extra-virgin olive
 oil, divided
2 cups water
1 cup einkorn berries
1 small yellow onion, diced
3 cloves garlic, sliced
1 pint cherry tomatoes, halved

1½ teaspoons kosher salt
¼ teaspoon red pepper flakes
¼ cup (¾ ounce) finely ground or
 shredded Parmesan cheese
2 cups (8 ounces) shredded
 mozzarella cheese
Easy Tomato Dipping Sauce (see
 page 83), for serving (optional)
Fresh basil leaves, for garnish

1   Preheat the oven to 400 degrees F.

2   Halve the eggplants lengthwise and brush the cut sides with 2 tablespoons of the olive oil. Set the eggplant halves cut side down on a parchment-lined baking sheet and roast for 30 minutes, until the insides are mushy. If they still have any firmness, return them to the oven for 3 or 4 minutes more. Set aside until they're cool enough to handle, about 10 minutes.

3   Meanwhile, make the filling: Put the water, einkorn, onion, garlic, cherry tomatoes, salt, red pepper flakes, and the remaining 1 tablespoon olive oil into a medium pot over high heat. Bring to a boil, then immediately decrease the heat to low and let it gently cook, uncovered, for 30 minutes. Check the water level and, if it still looks soupy, let it cook for 5 to 10 more minutes; watch it carefully to make sure the water doesn't evaporate completely, leaving the mixture to burn. Remove from the heat and stir in the Parmesan cheese. Set aside.

4   Scoop out most of the flesh of the eggplants, leaving enough so the eggplant halves hold their shape. If you have a hard time scooping them out, use a paring knife to make a crosshatch design in the center of the eggplant and scoop out just enough of the center to add some filling. Put the soft eggplant flesh into the einkorn mixture and stir to combine.

5   Line the eggplant halves up in a 9-by-13-inch casserole dish and divide the filling among them until they're full but not overstuffed. (If you have leftover filling, it makes a great side dish for another meal.)

6   Sprinkle the stuffed eggplant halves with the mozzarella to cover and bake for 15 minutes to warm everything and let the cheese melt and brown a little. If it's not browned, turn the broiler on for a few minutes to finish. Garnish with the fresh basil leaves and serve hot.

Breads

AND

Crackers

Everyday Einkorn Sandwich Bread

This is my everyday loaf. In my house we always have some on hand to use for morning toast and sandwiches, such as the grilled cheese on page 83. I recommend using sourdough starter, but if you don't have any, you can use yeast in the preferment instead. Make the preferment the night before you're going to mix the dough.

MAKES ONE 1-POUND LOAF

For the preferment
1 teaspoon well-fed sourdough
   starter, or ⅛ teaspoon instant yeast
½ cup water
½ cup (60 grams) whole grain
   einkorn flour

For the dough
1½ cups water
4 cups (480 grams) whole grain
   einkorn flour
2 teaspoons kosher salt

————

Butter or oil, for greasing the pan

1   To make the preferment, in a medium bowl, combine the sourdough starter (or yeast) with the water and flour and stir. Cover the mixture and let it sit at room temperature overnight or for at least 12 hours. When it's ready, the preferment will look bubbly.

2   To make the dough, pour the water into a large bowl. Add the preferment and mix it around a little. Add the flour and salt and mix until the flour is completely incorporated with no dry streaks or pockets. Cover the bowl with a dish towel and allow the dough to rest at room temperature for 30 minutes. Uncover the bowl and fold the dough inside the bowl: Reach under the dough and gently pull some up and over the top of the dough ball. Do this six to eight times, moving all the way around the dough ball. Cover the bowl and let it rest for another 30 minutes.

3   Grease the bottom and sides of a 1-pound (8½-by-4½-inch) loaf pan or a small (9-by-4-inch) pullman pan with butter. Set aside.

$\longrightarrow$

4   Wet a clean work surface by spreading around a little water. Place the dough on the surface and turn it so its surface is wet; this will keep it from sticking. With wet hands, form the dough into a loaf by rolling it up into a neat, tight log, jelly-roll style. Place it seam side down in the prepared pan. Cover with foil (or, if you're using a pullman pan, with the pan's lid) and let rest at room temperature for 1 hour. Move the covered pan into the fridge to proof for 18 hours.

5   About 20 minutes before baking, preheat the oven to 450 degrees F. Bake for 30 minutes, covered. Take off the lid or foil and cook, uncovered, for an additional 30 minutes. Let the loaf cool completely before delving in.

Bread Timing 101

Unless bread baking is part of your routine, it can be challenging to plan how this extended process can fit in with the rest of your schedule. Here's a sample schedule that shows how to work the steps in over the course of 3 days, ending with a fresh, fragrant, delicious loaf.

FRIDAY MORNING: Refresh the einkorn starter. (if using starter)
Friday night: Make the einkorn preferment and let it sit overnight.

SATURDAY MORNING: Mix the dough and ferment for 30 minutes. Stretch and fold the dough, then let it rest for another 30 minutes. Shape the dough and put it into the pan. Proof for 1 hour, then store it in the fridge overnight.

SUNDAY MORNING: Bake the bread!

Seedy Einkorn-Rye Bread

I used to go to a neighborhood bakery where they made the best tartine breakfast sandwiches (see sidebar, page 96). Because of them, I started making this loaf; it takes time but not too much work—the active parts take just a few minutes. Mostly it's just waiting. The rye makes this dough a little stiffer and stickier than a typical wheat bread dough, so if this is your first time working with it, don't be alarmed. Be sure to make the preferment the night before you're going to mix the dough. I proof this loaf for a long time in the fridge—there's some evidence that this makes the bread more digestible for people with gluten sensitivity. Even if the claim is overblown, it tastes good that way.

MAKES ONE 1-POUND LOAF

For the preferment
⅛ teaspoon instant yeast, or 1 teaspoon well-fed sourdough starter
½ cup water
½ cup (60 grams) whole grain einkorn flour

For the seed soaker
¼ cup pumpkin seeds
2 tablespoons flaxseed
2 tablespoons sesame seeds

½ cup boiling water

For the dough
1½ cups water
3 cups (375 grams) dark rye flour
1 cup (120 grams) whole grain einkorn flour
2 teaspoons kosher salt

————

Butter or oil for the pan

1   To make the preferment, in a medium bowl, combine the yeast (or sourdough starter) with the water and flour and stir. Cover the mixture and let it sit at room temperature overnight or for at least 12 hours. When it's ready, it will look bubbly.

2   To make the seed soaker, preheat the oven to 350 degrees F. Spread the pumpkin seeds, flaxseed, and sesame seeds in a single layer on a rimmed baking sheet and toast in the oven for 7 minutes. Put the toasted seeds in a small bowl and pour the boiling water over them. Cover and let rest overnight at room temperature.

3   To make the dough, pour the water into a large mixing bowl and stir in the active preferment, breaking it up a bit with your hands (don't worry about dissolving it completely into the water). Add the seed soaker, rye flour, einkorn flour, and salt and mix until the flour is completely incorporated with no dry streaks or pockets. Cover the bowl with a kitchen towel and allow the dough to rest at room temperature for 1 hour. The dough will rise somewhat, but it won't double in size like an all-wheat leavened loaf would.

4   Grease the bottom and sides of a 1-pound (8½-by-4½-inch) loaf pan or a small (9-by-4-inch) pullman pan with butter. Wet your hands to keep the dough from sticking to them and transfer the dough from the bowl into the pan. Gently press the dough into the pan so that it reaches into all the corners, using a bench scraper to coax it along if necessary. With a sharp knife, make two deep diagonal cuts in the top of the loaf. Let it rest on the counter, uncovered, for about 1 hour, then move it to fridge, loosely covered, to proof overnight, or about 18 hours.

5   About 20 minutes before baking, preheat the oven to 450 degrees F. I usually reinforce the diagonal cuts before putting it into the oven. Cover with foil (or, if you're using a pullman pan, with the pan's lid) and bake for 30 minutes. Lower the temperature to 350 degrees F, remove the lid or foil, and bake for 1 more hour. Let cool completely before slicing.

Tartine Sandwiches for the Win!

The seedy einkorn-rye loaves were inspired by one of my favorite bakeries of all time (sadly closed after the pandemic), which was known for its amazing tartine (open-faced) sandwiches. I want to put in a word for the workhorse that is a tartine sandwich. It will always come through in a pinch and on a dime for a satisfying meal seemingly out of the blue.

Think beans and greens on toast, for example. Or softly scrambled eggs and leftover roasted veggies piled on a thick slice with grainy mustard. The possibilities are endless.

To re-create the sandwich that inspired the seedy einkorn-rye loaf, spread a slice with goat cheese, top with slices of pickled beets and a fried egg, and shower with fresh dill.

Make-Ahead Einkorn Freezer Biscuits

If you like homemade biscuits but the thought of actually *making* homemade biscuits sends you running, this is the recipe for you. The dough is not as finicky as traditional buttermilk biscuits, so don't worry about baking up a batch of hockey pucks. Better still, you can freeze them and bake them straight from the freezer, meaning a fresh, hot biscuit is only ever twenty minutes away.

MAKES TWELVE 3-INCH OR EIGHTEEN 2-INCH BISCUITS

3½ cups (420 grams) whole grain einkorn flour, plus more to flour the work surface

1 tablespoon sugar

1 tablespoon baking powder

1 teaspoon kosher salt

½ cup sour cream

1¾ cups cold heavy cream

1   In a large mixing bowl, combine the flour, sugar, baking powder, and salt, and mix. Add the sour cream and stir with a wooden spoon until the mixture looks slightly shaggy. Gradually stir in the cream until it's incorporated and the mixture has come together and looks like a dough. Turn it out onto a floured surface and knead just a few turns; don't overwork. (The dough might be slightly sticky; it's okay to add more flour to the work surface to keep it from sticking too much.)

2   Line a baking sheet with parchment paper and set it beside your work surface. Pat the dough out until it's about ½ inch thick and cut into rounds or squares. For rounds, use a 2- or 3-inch biscuit cutter (or the rim of a glass), cutting as many as you can from the dough and transferring them to the prepared baking sheet (don't let them touch), then gathering the leftover dough, patting it out and cutting until all the dough is gone. For squares, pat the dough out into a rough rectangle and use a sharp knife to cut into 2-inch squares; transfer to the lined baking sheet.

3   Cover the pan loosely with plastic wrap or another baking sheet and freeze for at least 4 hours or overnight. When the biscuits are frozen, store them in a freezer bag; they will keep for up to 6 weeks.

4   To bake, preheat the oven to 400 degrees F. Set the frozen biscuits on a parchment- or silicone-lined baking sheet and bake for 20 minutes, rotating the pan halfway through. Serve hot.

Einkorn Focaccia

This is the simplest of all the breads in this book. It's versatile too—a canvas for various flavor combinations, from rosemary and salt to Parmesan and pepper and beyond. This forgiving dough can be tucked away in the fridge for up to a day before baking.

MAKES ONE 9-INCH ROUND LOAF

For the dough
2 cups (240 grams) whole grain
  einkorn flour
1 teaspoon kosher salt
1 teaspoon sugar
¾ teaspoon instant yeast
¾ cup water, plus more as needed
¼ cup extra-virgin olive oil, divided
Flake salt

For the optional toppings
1 cup (3½ ounces) shredded
  Parmesan cheese
2 cloves garlic, minced
Chopped leaves from 1 sprig
  rosemary (about 1 tablespoon)
¼ teaspoon sweet paprika
Coarsely ground black pepper

1   To make the dough, in a medium bowl, combine the einkorn flour, salt, sugar, and yeast and mix well.

2   In a large bowl, combine the water with 1 tablespoon of the olive oil (you'll use the rest to grease the pan). Add the dry ingredients to the wet and stir until the flour is totally incorporated into a soft dough. The consistency will be somewhere between a batter and a loose dough. If it's stiff at all, add another 2 or 3 tablespoons water. Cover the bowl with a kitchen towel and let the dough rest at room temperature for 15 minutes.

3   Wet your hands and loosen the dough from the sides of the bowl as you reach a hand under the mass and stretching it up to fold over itself. Turn the bowl a bit and do it again about eight times, until you've rotated the bowl all the way around. Cover with a kitchen towel and let rest for 15 minutes. Repeat this process three more times for a total of four cycles of 15-minute rests and folding the dough while rotating the bowl. After the last fold, cover the bowl and get your oven and pan ready while the dough rests.

4   Preheat the oven to 450 degrees F. Pour the remaining 3 tablespoons olive oil into the bottom of a 9-inch cake pan or pie plate and spread to coat. Sprinkle a pinch of flake salt over the oil.

5 Put the dough into the prepared pan, then turn it over so the whole mass of dough is coated in olive oil. Gently press the dough out to fill the pan; it's okay if the dough doesn't come all the way to the edges—you don't have to force it. Sprinkle a little more flake salt on top. If you want any toppings other than the salt, add them now. Let the dough rest for about 15 minutes before baking.

6 Bake for 25 minutes, until the top is golden brown and the edges are sizzling with olive oil. Let cool for about an hour before slicing (if you can wait that long). This loaf will stay fresh at room temperature for a day or two. It also freezes well, tightly wrapped in plastic wrap, for up to 1 month. To reheat, simply let it thaw, set it on a baking sheet, and crisp it up in a 350 degree F oven for about 10 minutes.

Versatile Pita Bread

My home is never without pita bread. Here's why: This most versatile of breads can act as a stand-in dinner roll; it can swaddle copious ingredients as a grab-and-go sandwich; it toasts well for breakfast; and, sliced into wedges and baked, leftover pitas can be transformed into pita chips for scooping up hummus or breaking up and throwing in a salad (see Note).

MAKES 8 PITAS

2 cups (240 grams) whole grain einkorn flour, plus more to flour the work surface and pan
1 teaspoon instant yeast

1 teaspoon kosher salt
¾ cup water, at room temperature
2 teaspoons extra-virgin olive oil

1   In a small bowl, stir together the flour, yeast, and salt.

2   In a large bowl, mix the water and olive oil, then add the flour mixture and mix with your hands until a shaggy dough forms. Cover the bowl with a plate or kitchen towel and let the dough rest at room temperature for 20 minutes.

3   Uncover the bowl and reach under the mass of dough, pulling some up and folding it onto itself. Turn the bowl and fold the dough four to six times, until you've turned the bowl all the way around. Cover and let rest for 20 minutes, then repeat, folding the dough and letting it rest for 20 minutes. Cover the bowl loosely with a kitchen towel and refrigerate overnight, or for about 12 hours. The dough will rise very slowly and ferment in the fridge.

4   Preheat the oven to 450 degrees F. If you have a pizza stone, put it in the oven to preheat. Alternatively, line a baking sheet with parchment paper and sprinkle it with flour. Set aside.

5   Remove the dough from the fridge and turn it out onto a floured work surface. Cut the dough into eight equal pieces, trying not to stretch the dough too much or tear it. Shape each piece into a round by folding the edges in and rolling each piece with your hands until you have a taut and smooth disk. As you work, place these on the baking sheet seam side down, not touching each other. Keep the dough pieces covered with a kitchen towel so they don't dry out too much.

6   To shape the pitas, sprinkle your work surface with plenty of flour to prevent sticking. Transfer a piece of dough to the floured surface and turn it over so its top is floured (so it won't stick to your hands). Use your hands to press each piece into a round about ¼ inch thick, then dust off the excess flour and transfer a few of them into the hot oven, either directly on a pizza stone or a few at a time on a parchment-lined baking sheet. Bake for 5 minutes; they will puff up, forming an internal pocket, and they will brown a bit. Turn them over and bake for another minute or so until both sides have a bit of a crust. Remove from the oven, transfer to a basket or wire rack, and cover with a towel to keep them warm. Shape and bake the pitas in small batches until they're all done.

7   Serve hot or at room temperature. Store at room temperature in a container with a little airflow.

NOTE: To make pita chips, preheat the oven to 400 degrees F. Cut the pita rounds into quarters, then open each like a book and tear or cut into two wedges. Brush a little olive oil onto each side, sprinkle with salt (and/ or garlic powder or paprika or whatever you fancy), and place on a baking sheet. Bake for 20 to 30 minutes, until a deep golden brown, flipping once or twice to ensure even baking.

Cheesy Sesame Crackers

I became obsessed with a particular kind of cheese cracker I found at a local specialty market. When I say *obsessed*, I actually mean something that looked more like an addiction. If I was passing even a block or two away, I'd swerve over and sneak in for more and more. Finally, I developed this recipe to satisfy my craving for that crunchy, savory snap I'd come to adore.

MAKES 3 TO 3½ DOZEN CRACKERS

1 cup (120 grams) whole grain einkorn flour
½ cup (2 ounces) shredded Parmesan cheese
½ cup sesame seeds
1 tablespoon sugar
¾ teaspoon sea salt
¼ teaspoon freshly ground black or white pepper
½ cup (1 stick) unsalted butter
1 egg, beaten

1   Preheat the oven to 350 degrees F. Line two baking sheets with parchment paper and set aside.

2   In the bowl of a food processor, combine the flour, Parmesan cheese, sesame seeds, sugar, salt, and pepper and pulse to combine. Cut the butter into four pieces and drop these in one by one; pulse until the dough looks crumbly. With the machine running, add the beaten egg and process until the dough comes together, about 1 minute.

3   Scoop out a tablespoon-size piece of dough (or a little less for a smaller cracker) and roll it into a ball in your hand. In your palm, flatten the ball into a small disk about ¼ inch thick and set it on the parchment-lined pan. Repeat with the rest of the dough, leaving 1 inch between each cracker on the pans.

4   Bake for 15 to 18 minutes, until golden in color and crispy at the edges. Let cool about 10 minutes before serving. To store, cool completely and keep in an airtight container for up to a week. You can also freeze the unbaked disks: Transfer the pans to the freezer for 10 minutes, then store the frozen disks tightly wrapped in plastic. Bake them right out of the freezer, on parchment-lined baking sheets.

Cheddar-and-Chive Snacking Loaf

This craveable loaf comes together quickly, and it's the perfect thing to have on hand when people in your household are foraging for a snack. If you're okay with corn, you can substitute cornmeal for a quarter of the flour and bake this in a 9-by-9-inch pan, like cornbread.

MAKES ONE 8-BY-4-INCH LOAF

2 cups (240 grams) whole grain
  einkorn flour
2 teaspoons kosher salt
1½ teaspoons baking powder
1 teaspoon sweet paprika
1 teaspoon mustard powder
½ teaspoon baking soda
½ teaspoon black pepper

1 cup (4 ounces) shredded
  cheddar cheese
¼ cup chopped chives
1 egg
1 cup buttermilk
¼ cup (½ stick) unsalted butter, melted,
  plus some softened butter for
  greasing the pan

1   Preheat the oven to 350 degrees F and grease an 8-by-4-inch loaf pan with softened butter.

2   In a large mixing bowl, whisk together the flour, salt, baking powder, paprika, mustard powder, baking soda, and black pepper. Stir in the cheese and chives. Set aside.

3   In a medium bowl, beat the egg, then mix in the buttermilk. Add the wet ingredients to the dry ingredients and stir together. Add the melted butter and stir until it's incorporated and no longer streaky. Don't overmix: As soon as everything that was dry is wet, it's done.

4   Scrape the batter into the prepared pan and place it on the middle rack of the oven. Bake for 40 to 45 minutes, turning the pan halfway through. You'll know it's done when the sides start to pull away from the pan and a toothpick inserted into the center comes out clean.

5   Let the loaf cool slightly in the pan, then turn it out onto a wire rack and let cool for about an hour before slicing. The bread will keep for about 5 days in a sealed bag (if it lasts that long). To store in the freezer, let the loaf cool completely, then wrap well and freeze for up to 2 months.

Under-an-Hour Cheater Bagels

I was skeptical about this recipe. I am a Jewish girl from Montreal and NYC, after all. But then I tried it, and honestly, it's a great way to get a packed-with-protein whole grain bagel. You still might visit a bagel shop occasionally, but this is a nice-to-have-on-hand healthy staple. Some cooks skip the step where you boil the dough before baking it, using an egg wash instead, but I like the quality that boiling adds. This recipe calls for full-fat yogurt, but I tested it with reduced-fat yogurt as well with good results.

MAKES 4 MEDIUM OR 6 SMALL BAGELS

1½ cups (180 grams) whole grain einkorn flour, plus more to flour the work surface

2 teaspoons baking powder

¾ teaspoon kosher salt

1¼ cups plain full-fat Greek yogurt

Sesame seeds, for topping (optional)

Everything bagel seasoning, for topping (optional)

1   Preheat the oven to 375 degrees F. Fill a large pot with water and set it over high heat to boil. Line a baking sheet with parchment paper or a silicone baking mat. Set aside.

2   In a medium bowl, combine the einkorn flour, baking powder, and salt and stir to mix well. Add the yogurt and stir to combine until a dough forms.

3   Turn the dough out onto a generously floured work surface and divide it into four or six pieces, depending on whether you want a regular-size bagel or a small one. Roll each piece of dough into a fat rope and then pinch the ends together to make a ring.

4   Ease the bagels into the boiling water one by one, without overcrowding the pot (work in batches if you need to). Boil for 1 minute or less per side; if they float immediately to the surface, turn them over so they boil on the other side. Don't overboil them, or they'll start to fall apart. With a spider or slotted spoon, transfer them to the baking sheet. Top with sesame seeds or everything bagel seasoning or leave plain.

5   Bake the bagels for 25 minutes, until golden. Transfer to a wire rack and let cool for about 10 minutes before serving.

Graham Crackers

These are 100 percent whole grain cracker-ish cookies, unlike store-bought graham crackers, which typically use a bit of whole grain to bolster a mostly white flour product. The snap when you bite into these is satisfying, and they are a yummy and wholesome after-school snack. You can also roll the dough out in big sheets to make cookie crumbs (which you can then use for the No-Bake Cheesecake Cups on page 121). Note that eggs and butter for this recipe need to be at room temperature before you use them, so take them out of the fridge a half hour before you'll need them.

MAKES 3 TO 4 DOZEN CRACKERS

1½ cups (180 grams) whole grain einkorn flour, plus more to flour the work surface

½ teaspoon baking powder

¼ teaspoon kosher salt

6 tablespoons (75 grams) packed brown sugar

¼ cup (½ stick) unsalted butter, at room temperature

1 egg, at room temperature

½ teaspoon vanilla extract

¼ teaspoon ground cinnamon (optional)

2 tablespoons whole milk (optional)

1   In a medium bowl, stir together the flour, baking powder, and salt. Set aside.

2   In the bowl of a stand mixer or in a large mixing bowl with an electric beater (or use a whisk), beat the brown sugar and butter on medium speed until they are well mixed and starting to gain volume, about 3 minutes in a stand mixer. Add the egg, vanilla extract, and cinnamon and beat on medium until well incorporated, 2 to 3 minutes. Add the flour mixture and beat on low speed until the dough forms a smooth, even mass. Use your hands to knead it in the bowl a few times to make sure it all comes together.

3   On a work surface, lay out a length of plastic wrap. Gather the dough in a ball and put it in the center of the plastic. Press the dough down until it's about ½ inch thick and fold the wrap around it to cover completely. Refrigerate for at least 2 hours and up to 1 day.

4   Preheat the oven to 350 degrees F. Line a baking sheet with parchment paper and set aside.

5   Remove the dough from the refrigerator, unwrap it, and cut it into two pieces; rewrap one piece and put it back in the fridge while you roll out the other piece. On a clean, lightly floured work surface, roll the dough out to a $\frac{1}{8}$- to $\frac{1}{16}$-inch thickness. If it's too stiff to roll, let it rest at room temperature for up to 10 minutes to soften.

6   Cut the crackers into whatever shape you like; I use either a 2-inch or a 3-inch round cookie cutter, but I've also cut these into squares with a fluted cutter. Place the cut dough on the parchment-lined baking sheet and dock each cracker by poking it with a fork about three times. Knead any scraps together and re-roll. (On the third re-roll, I usually don't cut but bake the remaining dough in one big sheet that I then crush into cookie crumbs.) For a shiny top, brush the cookies with a bit of the milk before baking.

7   Bake the crackers for 10 minutes, rotating the pan halfway through. Transfer the crackers to a rack to cool for about 10 minutes to get that snap that we expect when biting into a graham cracker. Eat immediately or store at room temperature in a sealed container for up to a month. To make cookie crumbs, pulse in a food processor until the crumbs are your desired consistency.

Tender Tortillas

Homemade tortillas are a game-changer: They will spoil you for the store-bought version. (You have been warned!)

MAKES EIGHT 6-INCH TORTILLAS

1 cup water
3 tablespoons avocado oil or
    unsalted butter

1 teaspoon kosher salt
2 cups (240 grams) whole grain
    einkorn flour

1 In a small pot over high heat, bring the water, oil, and salt to a rolling boil. Turn off the heat. Put the flour into a medium bowl and pour the still-hot liquid into it. Stir with a spatula until a ball of dough forms. Knead the dough inside the bowl once or twice, then cover the bowl with a kitchen towel and let the dough rest for 30 minutes.

2 On a clean work surface, cut the dough into eight pieces and form each into a ball. Cover the balls with a kitchen towel and let them rest for 30 more minutes.

3 Heat a frying pan or griddle over medium-high heat. Pat one ball of dough into a disk, then use a rolling pin to roll the dough from the center to the edges; rotate the dough as you work so the tortillas stay fairly round. Get it as thin as you can and then transfer to the hot pan. Cook for about 1 minute on the first side, until the bottom gets some color and the tortilla bubbles up a bit, then flip and cook for another minute on the other side. Don't overcook them or they'll get dry: The heat should be high enough that they cook quickly and don't dry out, so watch carefully and adjust the heat as necessary. Sometimes the first tortilla is a test run! Keep rolling the tortillas and cooking them one at a time (or two at a time if you're working on a big enough griddle).

$\longrightarrow$

4   Place the tortilla on a plate lined with a towel and cover the plate with an inverted bowl to keep the steam in so the tortillas stay flexible. As you finish each tortilla, stack it on top of the last one. If they get stiff before you're ready to fill them, put them in a steamer basket over boiling water (or in the microwave with a damp paper towel) for 30 seconds to make them flexible again. These will keep for up to 3 days in a sealed bag in the fridge.

10 Ways to Use Tortillas

1   **Breakfast burritos**: Make them ahead and freeze for a healthy breakfast on the go.

2   Smother with a bit of butter in a pan and use it to make a **crepe** by folding it around your favorite filling.

3   Make a batch of smaller tortillas and you have the perfect backdrop for classic tacos.

4   Use up bits and bobs in your fridge with **quesadillas**—some leftover veg, beans, bind it with some cheese, and you're good to go.

5   Don't have any einkorn bread on hand for that sandwich? Try making **wraps** with your leftover tortillas.

6   For a flourish, roll up a quick wrap and cut crosswise to make little **pinwheels**—also a good way to get kids eating more einkorn.

7   **Tortilla chips** make a great snack: Cut them and brush with a bit of olive oil, sprinkle with salt, and bake at 375 degrees F for 10 to 12 minutes.

8   Substitute leftover tortillas for no-bake noodles in a **lasagna**.

9   Layer about six tortillas with a meatball mixture (see page 79) spread between each tortilla, then cut into strips and skewer for a fun **kebab**. These are also great on the grill.

10 For a sweet treat, try brushing the tortillas with butter and sugar and toasting for an extra crunchy **cinnamon toast**.

Sweet Treats

Cake-Doughnut Cake

I'm not a doughnut person, but I do love the flavor of a cake donut, so I made a cake donut into a full cake. If that sounds confusing, make it and hopefully you'll see what I mean. Basically, this will satisfy doughnut and cake people alike. Lovers of both may just be in heaven. Since the eggs will need to be at room temperature for this recipe, take them out of the fridge at least a half hour before you'll need them.

MAKES ONE 8-INCH CAKE

For the cake
½ cup (1 stick) unsalted butter, at room temperature, plus more for the pan
1¾ cups (210 grams) whole grain einkorn flour
½ teaspoon fine salt
1½ teaspoons baking powder
¼ teaspoon baking soda
¾ cup (135 grams) granulated sugar
2 eggs, at room temperature

1 cup sour cream
2 teaspoons freshly grated nutmeg
2 teaspoons vanilla extract

For the glaze
1 cup confectioners' sugar
Pinch of kosher salt
3 to 4 tablespoons whole milk

———

2 tablespoons melted butter, for brushing the cake top

1   To make the cake, preheat the oven to 350 degrees F. Prepare an 8-inch round cake pan by greasing the sides with a little butter and lining the bottom with an 8-inch circle of parchment paper (it's okay to skip the paper if you don't have parchment paper on hand).

2   In a medium bowl, whisk together the flour, salt, baking powder, and baking soda. Set aside.

3   In the bowl of a stand mixer, or in a large bowl with an electric hand mixer or a spoon, beat together the sugar and eggs on medium speed until well combined and becoming light and airy, about 2 minutes in a stand mixer. Add the sour cream, butter, nutmeg, and vanilla, and mix until smoothly combined.

4   Add the dry ingredients to the wet ingredients a little bit at a time, in about three batches, mixing well on low until the batter is smooth.

5   Pour the batter into the prepared pan and bake for about 30 minutes, until the top of the cake is golden and has a slight dome shape and the sides start to pull away from the pan a bit. When you insert a toothpick, it should come out clean. Remove from the oven and set on a rack to cool for about 10 minutes.

6   To make the glaze, in a small bowl, whisk together the confectioners' sugar, salt, and 3 tablespoons of the milk to make the glaze. If it's not quite thin enough to be brushed over the cake, whisk in some or all of the final 1 tablespoon of milk.

7   To finish the cake, remove the cake from the pan by inverting the pan over a pretty serving plate. Gently brush the top with the melted butter, followed by the glaze.

No-Bake Cheesecake Cups

Making a traditional cheesecake takes a lot of steps: a lot of baking and a lot of waiting for it to set. And if you're not feeding a crowd, you're often left with a huge amount of leftover cake. I developed this recipe to solve for some of this—think of these as an everyday-friendly version of cheesecake. There's no baking, and because they're small, they're set and ready to eat in about an hour.

MAKES 1 DOZEN CHEESECAKE CUPS

For the crust
1 cup crumbled Graham Crackers (page 111), or 4 ounces of store-bought graham crackers, crushed
3 tablespoons sugar
Pinch of kosher salt
¼ cup (½ stick) unsalted butter, melted

For the filling
1 pound cream cheese, softened
1 cup sugar
⅛ teaspoon kosher salt
2 tablespoons sour cream
2 teaspoons freshly squeezed lemon juice
1 teaspoon vanilla extract
1 cup heavy cream
Sliced fresh fruit, for serving

1   Line a twelve-cup muffin tin with liners.

2   To make the crust, in a food processor, pulse the crumbled graham crackers, sugar, and salt until well mixed. Drizzle in the melted butter and process until well combined; test by pinching some of the crumb mixture—if it holds together, it's ready to use. Spoon about 1 tablespoon of the crumb mixture into each lined muffin cup, adding a little more to each as needed to use all the crumb mix. Press the back of the tablespoon into each cup to compact the crumb base; this will help it hold together. Refrigerate while you make the filling.

3 To make the filling, combine the cream cheese, sugar, and salt in a mixing bowl and beat it with a hand mixer (or use a stand mixer) on medium speed for a minute or two, until the sugar and salt grains are evenly incorporated into the cream cheese. Add the sour cream, lemon juice, and vanilla extract and beat until smooth, about 1 minute. Add the heavy cream and beat until everything comes together in a smooth, airy mixture, about 2 minutes. (If you're using a stand mixer, switch to the whisk attachment when you add the cream.)

4 Retrieve the muffin tin from the refrigerator. Evenly divide the cheesecake filling among the cups, spooning it in and smoothing the top. (If you have a piping bag, you can use it to fill the cups, or put the filling into a quart-size plastic bag and cut the corner to use it as a piping bag.)

5 Put the tin back in the refrigerator to set the cheesecake cups. This will take about an hour, but the longer it sets the better the texture, so feel free to hold them for several hours.

6 To serve, peel back the muffin liner from the custard (leave the bottom in place to help contain the crumbs) and set on a dessert plate; top with a little fresh fruit.

Summer Berry Galette

This recipe makes two disks of dough, enough for two galettes; you can use them both or freeze one disk, tightly wrapped in plastic, for later. To make one galette at a time, just halve the filling ingredients. If you prefer to make the dough with a food processor rather than a pastry cutter, feel free.

MAKES 2 GALETTES, SERVING 8 TO 12

For the dough
2 cups (240 grams) whole grain
   einkorn flour
½ teaspoon kosher salt
½ teaspoon sugar
¾ cup (1½ sticks) cold unsalted
   butter, cut into pieces
6 to 8 tablespoons ice water

For the filling
3 cups fresh or frozen summer
   berries, such as blueberries, sliced
   strawberries, and/or raspberries

½ cup sugar
2 tablespoons cornstarch
1 tablespoon freshly squeezed
   lemon juice
Pinch of kosher salt
For finishing and serving:
1 egg
1 teaspoon water
2 tablespoons sanding or
   demerara sugar
Vanilla ice cream, for serving

1   To make the dough, in a large bowl, combine the flour, salt, and sugar. Use a pastry cutter to cut about three-quarters of the cold butter pieces into the flour mixture until it looks a little shaggy (while you're doing this, keep the rest of the butter in the fridge so it stays cold). Cut the remaining butter pieces in until the dough looks sandy, with some larger butter pieces remaining. Add the ice water 1 tablespoon at a time, incorporating with your hands, until the dough just comes together; squeeze the dough gently and if it sticks to itself, you're done. Transfer to a clean work surface and knead once or twice, then cut the dough in half and press each half into a disk. Wrap each disk in plastic wrap and refrigerate at least 1 hour and up to 3 days (or freeze for up to 1 month).

2   To prepare the galette, preheat the oven to 375 degrees F. Set two baking sheets aside on a work surface.

→

3   To make the filling, put the berries in a large mixing bowl with the sugar, cornstarch, lemon juice, and salt. If you are using frozen berries, they can come directly from the freezer—no need to thaw.

4   On a clean work surface, roll out each disk and transfer one to each baking sheet. Place half the filling ingredients in the middle of each disk of dough, leaving about 1½ inches of dough clear around the edges. Fold the edges of the dough in to partially cover the berries and to create a crust that will hold the ingredients as the galette bakes. Leave a circle of berries peeking out in the center.

5   To finish, make an egg wash by beating the egg with the teaspoon of water in a small bowl. Brush the top of the galette dough with egg wash and sprinkle everything with sanding sugar.

6   Bake for 30 minutes, rotating the pans halfway through. Slice the galettes while hot and serve with a scoop of vanilla ice cream on top.

Einkorn "Rice" Pudding

Rice pudding is a deeply comforting treat, and trading the rice for einkorn adds a distinctive golden sweetness and a big fiber boost. The secret to coaxing a creamy texture out of einkorn is to put the berries in a blender and crack them a bit. I spoon this pudding into mismatched teacups and serve it with Graham Crackers (page 111) on the side for a little crunch. It also works great as a lunchbox treat!

MAKES 4 SERVINGS

1 cup einkorn berries
3 cups whole milk
½ cup sugar
¼ teaspoon kosher salt

½ vanilla bean, split lengthwise, or
  1 teaspoon vanilla bean paste
2 tablespoons unsalted butter

1   Place the einkorn berries in a blender or food processor and pulse several times, just until the einkorn berries crack open a little—don't let it turn into flour.

2   In a medium saucepan, combine the cracked einkorn berries, whole milk, sugar, salt, and vanilla bean. Bring the mixture to a simmer over medium-low heat and cover. Simmer, stirring occasionally, for 35 minutes, until the pudding thickens up and becomes almost syrupy. If it still looks thin, let it cook a bit longer.

3   Pull out the vanilla bean and stir in the butter to melt and combine. Serve warm. If you have leftover pudding, store it in a sealed container in the fridge for up to 3 days.

Honey-Wheat-Peach Frozen Yogurt

This recipe uses no refined sugar, relying solely on fruit and honey for sweetening. The sweet chewiness of the einkorn berries adds texture and that little something special. This frozen yogurt can be made in an ice-cream maker if you have one, but you don't need one.

MAKES 1 QUART

¼ cup einkorn berries
½ cup plus 1 tablespoon honey, divided
1 pound frozen or fresh peaches
1¼ cups whole-milk plain Greek yogurt

1 tablespoon freshly squeezed lemon juice
1 tablespoon vanilla extract
½ teaspoon almond extract
¼ teaspoon kosher salt

1   If you're using an ice-cream maker, pre-freeze the bowl. If you're not using an ice-cream maker, put a 2-quart lidded container in the freezer to chill while you make the yogurt mixture.

2   In a small saucepan over high heat, bring 3 inches of water to a boil. Add the einkorn berries, making sure that the water is covering the berries by at least 2 inches. Cook, uncovered, for 25 minutes, then drain. Transfer the hot einkorn berries to a small bowl, add 1 tablespoon of the honey, and stir to coat the einkorn with it. Set aside to cool.

3   Meanwhile, if you're using fresh peaches and want to peel them, fill a 3-quart pot about three-quarters full with water and place over high heat to boil. Set a big bowl of ice water near the stove. Cut an X into the skin at the bottom of each peach and put them into the boiling water for about 2 minutes, until the skin around the X starts to peel away. Remove the fruit from the boiling water and place in the bowl of ice water to halt the cooking. The skins should peel easily at this point. Peel and pit the peaches and cut the flesh into chunks.

4   Put the fresh or frozen peaches, yogurt, remaining ½ cup of honey, lemon juice, vanilla, almond extract, and salt in the bowl of a food processor or blender and mix on high until well blended, a minute or two. I like to stop short of making a puree, leaving a few chunks of fresh peach in the finished frozen yogurt, but you decide. Add the honeyed einkorn to the mixture and stir to disperse.

5   If you're using an ice-cream maker, scrape the mixture into it and process according to the manufacturer's instructions. It takes about 45 minutes in mine. Don't let it overprocess: Remove it when it's starting to look dense, just past the soft-serve stage.

6   If you don't have an ice-cream maker, scrape the peach–honey–einkorn mixture into your pre-chilled lidded container, cover, and put it back in the freezer for 30 minutes. Open the container and stir well, then return it to the freezer. Stir every 30 to 45 minutes, until it's frozen to your liking.

7   You can serve the yogurt immediately as a soft, icy treat, but it will really shine if you freeze it for at least 3 more hours.

8   Store in an airtight container in the freezer for up to a month. If you have some parchment paper, set a piece on top of the yogurt to prevent freezer burn—though honestly you probably won't keep it around long enough for that to be an issue.

Date-Pecan Bars

These are in the same lunchbox category as old-fashioned granola bars and cereal bars: just something a little sweet that's still wholesome. Serve these warm or at room temperature with a tall glass—or carton—of milk!

MAKES 1 DOZEN BARS

Softened unsalted butter, for greasing the pan
1 cup (3½ ounces) pecan halves
2 cups (240 grams) whole grain einkorn flour
½ cup rolled oats
½ cup (100 grams) packed brown sugar
1 teaspoon ground cinnamon

½ teaspoon kosher salt
½ cup (1 stick) unsalted butter, melted
2 cups (10 ounces) pitted medjool dates
1 cup water
¼ cup granulated sugar
1 tablespoon freshly squeezed lemon juice

1   Preheat the oven to 350 degrees F. Grease the bottom and sides of an 8-by-8-inch brownie pan with butter. (If you like, cut an 8-by-16-inch piece of parchment to fit across the bottom and two sides of your pan with some overhang for easy removal. I often make these in a glass dish and store them in it, cutting pieces out as desired.)

2   Put the pecans in a baking pan and toast in the oven for 8 minutes to make them a little crispy and let them develop a deep, roasty flavor. Remove from the oven and let them cool a bit, then chop them into small pieces and set aside.

3   In a large mixing bowl, combine the flour, rolled oats, brown sugar, cinnamon, and salt and mix well. Add the melted butter and stir until everything is well combined. Spoon half of this mixture into the bottom of the prepared pan, spread it out, and press it down to form the crust. Put the rest of the mixture into the fridge until you're ready to top the date bars. Put the pan in the oven and parbake the crust for about 10 minutes, until it's just starting to get crisp. Remove from the oven and let it cool while you cook the dates.

→

4   If the dates are large, chop them roughly to make small pieces. Put them in a small pot and add the water and granulated sugar. Bring to a boil over high heat. Immediately turn it down to a simmer and cover. Return to the pot every so often and stir, keeping an eye on the dates until they break down and become soft, 20 to 25 minutes. Remove from the heat and add the lemon juice and half of the chopped roasted pecans.

5   Spread the date filling on top of the parbaked crust, then retrieve the topping mixture from the refrigerator. Add the rest of the pecans to the topping and stir to disperse, then sprinkle this mixture onto the date filling.

6   Bake for 25 minutes, until the top is crumbly and the dates are set. Let cool on a rack for at least 15 minutes, but if you can wait longer, you'll get a cleaner cut when you slice the bars. Serve warm or store in a lidded container at room temperature for up to a week.

Classic Brownies

I like my brownies a little on the cakey side, but these still have a bit of fudginess in the center and a glossy top.

MAKES ONE 8-BY-8-INCH PAN OF BROWNIES

Softened unsalted butter, for
  greasing the pan
¾ cup (85 grams) cocoa powder
½ cup (60 grams) whole grain
  einkorn flour
½ teaspoon kosher salt
½ teaspoon baking powder

3 eggs
1½ cups (270 grams) sugar
2 teaspoons vanilla extract
½ cup (1 stick) unsalted butter,
  melted
1 tablespoon sunflower or other
  neutral oil

1   Preheat the oven to 325 degrees F. Grease the bottom of an 8-by-8-inch brownie pan with butter.

2   In a medium bowl, sift (or stir) together the cocoa powder, flour, salt, and baking powder. Set aside.

3   In a large bowl, whisk the eggs until they're a little foamy. (If you'd prefer, you can use an electric hand mixer or a stand mixer.) Add the sugar and beat until the mixture looks a little ribbony: It will leave trails that slowly fill in as you mix. Stir in the vanilla extract.

4   In a small bowl, mix together the melted butter and oil and drizzle this slowly into the egg mixture and beat until emulsified. Stir in the flour mixture and mix until you have a smooth, even batter with no streaks or pockets of dry flour. Scrape it into the prepared brownie pan and level out the top. Bake on the middle rack of the oven and for 45 minutes, turning halfway through the cooking time, until a toothpick inserted into the center comes out clean. Let the brownies cool in the pan for 10 minutes to set before cutting into them.

Tahini Tea Biscuits

I like peanut butter, but I love tahini. This recipe is inspired by some peanut butter cookies I once had at a bakery that were just barely held together by the other ingredients. They were heaven when dipped into a warm beverage. Here is my ideal of an afternoon treat, and it comes together in less than a half hour. Since the egg will need to be at room temperature for this recipe, take it out of the fridge at least a half hour ahead of time.

MAKES 2 DOZEN BISCUITS

1 cup tahini
½ cup (1 stick) unsalted
    butter, softened
½ cup (90 grams) granulated sugar
¼ cup (50 grams) packed brown sugar

1 egg, at room temperature
1½ cups (180 grams) whole grain
    einkorn flour
1 teaspoon baking powder

1   Preheat the oven to 350 degrees F and prepare two baking sheets with parchment paper or silicone baking mats.

2   In the bowl of a stand mixer, combine the tahini, butter, granulated sugar, and brown sugar. Beat on medium speed until well mixed, 1 to 2 minutes. (Alternatively, mix in a large bowl with a spoon or an electric hand mixer.) Add the egg and mix until combined, then add the flour and baking powder and mix on low until a dough forms. There's no need to overmix—just stop when everything is combined.

3   Use a tablespoon to spoon dollops of dough onto the prepared baking sheets and place them in the oven, one on each of two racks (or freeze the balls for later; see Note). Bake for 18 to 22 minutes, rotating the pans halfway through the cooking time so they bake evenly. The cookies are done when they look crispy and lightly golden at the edges.

4   Store at room temperature for up to a week if you have any left over.

NOTE: To freeze raw cookie dough balls, spoon the dollops of dough onto a single baking sheet and put it in the freezer for 10 minutes to flash freeze, then store the dough balls in an airtight container in the freezer for up to 2 months. Bake directly from the freezer, adding 2 minutes to the baking time.

Skillet Chocolate Chip Cookie

What's better than a warm chocolate chip cookie straight from the oven? Well, one really big chocolate chip cookie that's gooey on the inside and crisp at the edges and everyone can get their own spoon and dig in collectively. I always go for the edges, while my husband concentrates on the middle. Of course, if you don't want to share, you can cut it in slices and serve it more like a blondie.

MAKES 1 GIANT COOKIE

1¾ (210 grams) cups whole grain einkorn flour
¾ teaspoon baking soda
¾ teaspoon kosher salt
½ cup (1 stick) unsalted butter, softened

½ cup (100 grams) packed brown sugar
½ cup (90 grams) granulated sugar
1 egg
2 teaspoons vanilla extract
¾ cup dark chocolate chips
1 cup chopped pecans

1   Preheat the oven to 350 degrees F.

2   In a medium bowl, mix together the flour, baking soda, and salt. Set aside.

3   In a large bowl, beat the butter, brown sugar, and granulated sugar with an electric hand mixer until it's a little fluffy, about 5 minutes. Add the egg and vanilla and beat until everything is well incorporated, about 1 minute. Stir in the chocolate chips and pecans.

4   Scrape the batter into a 10- or 12-inch cast-iron skillet. The 10-inch skillet will make a thicker cookie that stays chewier in the center—the edges will be crisp and buttery no matter which pan you use.

5   Bake for 20 to 25 minutes, until golden brown. Let the cookie cool for 10 minutes or so, then cut it in the pan and serve the slices.

Resources

These are the places I turn to for high-quality flour. This is certainly not an exhaustive list, and I encourage you to try others that may be grown in your area. Buying a diversity of locally grown grains helps not only your health but also our soils and crop rotations.

Whole Grain Einkorn and Berries
- Bluebird Grain Farms | BluebirdGrainFarms.com
- Barton Springs Mill | BartonSpringsMill.com
- Camas Country Mill | CamasCountryMill.com
- Carolina Ground | CarolinaGround.com
- Janie's Mill | JaniesMill.com
- Maine Grains | MaineGrains.com

For All-Purpose (Not Whole Grain) Einkorn Flour
- Grand Teton Ancient Grains | AncientGrains.com
- Jovial Foods | JovialFoods.com

For Einkorn Pasta
- Jovial Foods | JovialFoods.com
- Sfoglini | Sfoglini.com

For Reading More About Einkorn
- *Restoring Heritage Grains* by Eli Rogosa
  This book introduced me to einkorn and is an important book about why it matters to eat and grow ancient grains.

Acknowledgments

To Sonya Sanford for always meeting up for coffee dates at the farmers' market. I love perusing seasonal delights together and then sitting in the park to share ideas and exchange hugs. You always see more in me than I see in myself, and when you point the way, it's always been right. You're brilliant and I love everything you do.

To Andrew Ross and Anomarel Ogen, both for being the most fun to nerd out on grain knowledge with. You have deep wisdom about grain, and you teach and inspire. When you mention facts in passing, I'm listening.

Emily Park for being a friend and colleague and the person I can call to talk through a recipe. She's also the best chef I've ever worked with, hands down. I trust her palate and her sensibilities.

Marnee Horesh for always having a kind word to say—championing me along, tasting lots of food, and creating community when I needed it most.

To Jill Saginario for being such a clear and consistent voice. Books are really written by a team, and a good editor makes it all more collaborative and worthwhile.

To my family for being the people I always come home to. We gather around the crazy time-lapse of a kitchen counter, where our life happens. Thank you for meeting there these past months to eat plates and plates of food made of einkorn and give feedback. If I didn't have you people to eat with, none of this would be worth it.

Finally, to all the women throughout time—the mothers, grandmothers, and aunties—who did the strong, resilient work of feeding and caring for us to bring us to this moment we live today. These are the people who didn't get accolades for doing the care work that makes everything else possible. They deserve our respect and admiration. It's why, to change the world, all you really need to do is offer them your seat and think of them every time you eat this ancient grain.

Index

T

Printed in Colombia

SASQUATCH BOOKS with colophon is a registered trademark of Blue Star Press, LLC

29 28 27 26 25   9 8 7 6 5 4 3 2 1

The authorized representative in the EU for product safety and compliance is Authorised Rep Compliance Ltd., Ground Floor, 71 Lower Baggot Street, Dublin D02 P593, Ireland. www.arccompliance.com

Text: Adrian J. S. Hale
Editor: Jill Saginario
Production editor: Peggy Gannon
Photography: Dina Avila
Stylist: Anne Parker
Designer: Tony Ong

Library of Congress Cataloging-in-Publication Data is available.

The recipes contained in this book have been created for the ingredients and techniques indicated. Neither publisher nor author is responsible for your specific health or allergy needs that may require supervision. Nor are publisher and author responsible for any adverse reactions you may have to the recipes contained in the book, whether you follow them as written or modify them to suit your personal dietary needs or tastes.

ISBN: 978-1-63217-601-1

Sasquatch Books
1325 Fourth Avenue, Suite 1025
Seattle, WA 98101

SasquatchBooks.com